THE
ideals
WHOLE GRAIN COOKBOOK

This book, we believe, brings together a collection of recipes using whole grain foods that represents the very best of the best . . .

combining nutrition and good flavor, we have added a little bit of poetry and prose, a quotation or two, a touch of photography and art . . .

hoping to make your adventure into whole grain cooking and baking an *ideal* experience

. . . which will result in many enjoyable, delicious and nutritious meals for you to prepare . . . and for those near and dear to you to enjoy.

ISBN 0-89542-626-9 250
IDEALS PUBLISHING CO., MILWAUKEE, WIS. 53201
© COPYRIGHT MCMLXXIII, PRINTED AND BOUND IN U.S.A.

Seventh Printing

CONTENTS

GRAINS OF WHEAT

Have you ever held within your hand
Little grains of wheat
And wondered how these tiny seeds
Brought many things to eat?

Sometimes a biscuit, or a roll,
A loaf of bread, pastry or cake;
Sometimes a cereal, hot or cold,
Or a tender, hot, brown pancake.

But before they are any of these
They are a green carpet in spring,
That turns with magical quietness
Into golden plumes that swing.

For beauty is spread across the land
By small grains of wheat,
And bounty is spread across the board
In delicious things to eat.

Belle Banister Broadbent

ABOUT WHOLE WHEAT

Because most of us need to cut down on calories, it is important that the calories we do eat are not empty ones. Flour ground from the whole grain and grown on fertile soil is a big step toward nutrition. If the right flour is used, the following recipes will make delicious foods.

Be sure that the flour is finely ground from high protein or hard wheat. Whole wheat flours are not as uniform as white flour, but come in all grades of coarseness. The recipes in this book are designed for whole wheat flour fine enough to go through a coarse sieve or sifter . . . bran, germ, and all. (Don't use a double sifter because some of the bran will get caught between the two screens.)

If you use a coarser flour, you will have to adjust the recipe. You may succeed, but the results will not be as good as with finely ground flour.

Because soft wheat flour contains less gluten than hard wheat, it will make a good cake but not good yeast bread. However, whole wheat flour ground from hard wheat is good in any recipe in this book.

HELPFUL HINTS

After grains are ground (before and after baking), they are best refrigerated. This preserves the flavor, nutrition, and freshness.

These recipes designate whether to stir or to sift the flour. Packed-down flour is loosened by stirring. Sifting into a measuring cup makes a difference of over 2 T. less flour per cup than stirring. This may make a real difference in a recipe.

Ovens vary in temperature—watch any new recipe to see when it is done.

Glass pans bake faster than metal pans.

If you want to increase the protein value of your baked foods, substitute 1 to 2 T. soy flour for an equal amount of WW flour.

Use nested measuring cups for dry ingredients. Sift the flour into the cup, scraping off the excess with a knife for accurate measurement.

Marked glass measuring cups are best for liquids; they are less likely to spill. I have found a few sifters that won't sift whole wheat flour. The handle that you squeeze is one kind.

If you prefer honey instead of sugar, replace each cup of sugar with an equal amount of honey and reduce the liquid by ¼ c. For example, in the bread recipe, use ⅓ c. honey in place of the brown sugar and use 1⅓ T. less of water.

Egg whites at room temperature beat up larger than if they are cold.

Use large eggs for these recipes. If they are small, add an extra egg for every 2 to 4 eggs.

Cold retards and heat kills baking yeast. It thrives in a warm temperature. Keeping the dough covered with a towel (cloth or paper) in a warm place helps insure a light loaf of bread.

Three Hints That Shorten Kneading Time

Let dough rise once before kneading.

Cook part of flour with liquid, stirring constantly until smooth and thick.

Knead this way: Press down on dough, then fold in half and press down again. Repeat this until dough becomes smooth and elastic.

BASIC STONE MILL BREAD

Mix ½ c. warm water, 1 T. brown sugar or honey, and 1½ pkgs. dry yeast. Set side. Good, active yeast will double in size by the time you are ready to mix it into the dough.

Mix 1 c. stirred WW flour with 1½ c. water. Cook until thick and smooth, stirring constantly. This mixture will be lumpy at first and will stick to the pan, but if you keep on cooking and stirring, it will smooth out. Then put the mixture into a large bowl.

Add to the cooked flour in the following order: ¼ c. mild-flavored honey or ⅓ c. well-packed brown sugar, 1 scant T. salt, ⅓ c. powdered milk, ⅓ c. oil, 1 egg, and 1 c. stirred WW flour. Mix well. (If you use noninstant powdered milk, mix with the flour to prevent lumping.)

Add yeast mixture to flour mixture, which by now should be cool enough not to kill the yeast but warm enough to help it grow.

Add 2½ c. stirred WW flour to the above. If you have used honey instead of sugar, add another 2 T. WW flour. Mix well. The dough should be almost stiff enough to hold its shape.

Leave dough in the bowl, covering it with a towel and placing it in a warm, nondrafty place for about 1 hour, or until doubled in bulk. Turn out onto floured board, table, or cookie sheet. Knead 2 to 3 minutes or until smooth and elastic, using just enough flour to keep the dough from sticking to your hands. In kneading, push the dough away from you with the heel of your hand. Then pull the top of the dough over toward you, folding the dough. Now press down and away again. This folding action stretches the gluten, giving a good texture to the bread. Again cover the dough with a towel, and let stand 15 minutes. Knead the bread a few strokes, then cut it into 8 equal pieces and let stand another 15 minutes. (If you are in a hurry, you can leave out the two 15-minute rest periods; however, the texture of your bread will suffer.)

Now, treat each piece of dough this way: Press flat, fold together several times, then roll with the hands to make a cylinder about 1-inch thick. Braid 4 cylinders together for each loaf, starting at the center of the loaf and working to each end. (To braid 4 at a time, weave the cylinder that is on the right side under, over, and under the other 3, until it is on the left side. Then take the new one that is on the right side, and work it under, over, and under. Continue this way.) It takes 4 strips to make a pretty loaf. Pinch the ends together and tuck under. Place on greased cookie sheet, cover with a towel, and let rise until puffy, about double. If desired, you may brush lightly with beaten egg and sprinkle with sesame or poppy seeds. Bake at 375° for 30 to 35 minutes. This bread will be moist when baked.

Loaf pans: You can use loaf pans, but it is still a good idea to braid the dough, as the texture will be better. It also needs to be baked longer in loaf pans.

Round loaves: Tiny loaves baked on a cookie sheet is one of the secrets of good whole wheat bread. They rise better. I often make 4 tiny round loaves from 1 recipe. To make each loaf, fold the dough and press together until you have a tight loaf, tucking the ends under and pinching together.

Mixers: You can use an electric rotary mixer, until the dough gets too thick. If you plan to make several recipes at one time, a bread mixer is a great help.

Storing bread: Keep bread in the refrigerator in an airtight container. This protects the flavor and freshness. You can also freeze it. Slice before freezing, then thaw just the amount you want to use.

RYE BREAD

2 T. caraway seeds may be added to the basic Stone Mill Bread recipe.

Substitute 1½ c. rye flour for 1½ c. WW flour, adding rye flour at the end.

When you are ready to shape the loaves, make 2 long ones. Sprinkle greased cookie sheet with a little cornmeal and place the loaves on it. When the loaves have risen, brush them with beaten egg and make shallow diagonal cuts on the top of the loaves with a sharp knife. Bake.

ANISE BREAD

Add 2 T. anise seed to Stone Mill Bread recipe. This is delicious served with a mixture of butter and honey.

POTATO BREAD

Make these changes in the Stone Mill Bread recipe: Scrub 1 medium potato, cut up and put into a blender with the 1½ c. water in the recipe. Liquefy. Mix with the flour and cook as usual.

Shape into 4 small loaves and bake on greased cookie sheet.

GARLIC BREAD

Add 3 to 5 cloves of crushed garlic to the Stone Mill Bread recipe, depending on your taste for garlic and on the size of the cloves.

CELERY BREAD

Add 2 T. celery seed to Stone Mill Bread recipe.

ONION BREAD

Make these changes in the Stone Mill Bread recipe: Measure 2 c. chopped onions. Reduce the water in the recipe to 1 c. and put into a blender with the onions. Liquefy. Mix with the 1 c. WW flour and cook as usual.

Shape into 4 small loaves and bake on greased cookie sheet.

FRUIT-NUT BREAD

Make Stone Mill Bread dough, adding the juice of one lemon (if desired) while mixing. When ready to shape, divide into 3 loaves and treat as follows:

For each loaf use ⅓ c. chopped dates, ⅓ c. raisins, and ⅓ c. pecans. Flatten dough to a rectangle. Put half of the fruit and nuts on one half of the rectangle and sprinkle with cinnamon. Fold the other half over and seal the edges. Flatten out again and repeat. Shape into a round loaf by tucking the edges under snugly. Place on greased cookie sheet to rise until double. Bake at 375° for about 40 minutes. Ice while still hot with a thin powdered sugar and water icing.

RAISIN BREAD

Make like Fruit-Nut Bread, leaving out lemon, dates, and nuts but doubling the raisins.

> Rye Bread and Anise Bread doughs make excellent sweet rolls.

FRENCH BREAD

Mix together ½ c. warm water, 1 T. honey or brown sugar, and 1½ pkgs. dry yeast. Set aside.

Mix 1 c. water with 2/3 c. stirred WW flour. Cook, stirring constantly, until thick and smooth. Place in mixing bowl.

Add to the cooked flour 2 T. oil, 1½ tsp. salt, 2 egg whites, and 1 c. stirred WW flour, mixing well. Then add yeast mixture and another 1¼ c. stirred WW flour.

Cover and let rise in mixing bowl until doubled. Turn out onto floured board and knead until smooth and elastic. Cover and let stand 15 minutes. Cut in half and shape into oblong loaves. Grease cookie sheets and sprinkle cornmeal where you place the loaves. Let rise until doubled, then gently brush with egg white and make shallow slits diagonally across loaves with a sharp knife.

Place pan of hot water on bottom shelf of oven.

Bake at 400° for about 40 minutes. Cool on cake rack.

HARD ROLLS

Make French Bread dough. When ready to shape, make into 1 dozen rolls, placing on greased cookie sheets. Let rise until doubled, brush with egg white, and sprinkle with poppy seeds if desired.

Place pan of hot water on bottom shelf of oven.

Bake at 400° for about 25 minutes.

CLOVER LEAF ROLLS

Use the Stone Mill Bread recipe. Instead of using flour for kneading, use oil, kneading on a nonporous surface. Shape dough into 1-inch balls. Place 3 balls into each greased muffin cup. Let rise until double, then bake at 400° for about 15 minutes. Let stand 3 to 5 minutes for easier removal from muffin cups.

You may shape these rolls in any favorite way. Or brush with egg and sprinkle with poppy or sesame seed just before baking.

CHEESE BREAD

Make Stone Mill Bread dough and divide into 3 parts. Flatten each part, dot half of the dough with ⅓-inch cubes of American cheese, fold the other half over, repeat, then tuck edges under until you have a round loaf. Place loaves on a greased cookie sheet and let rise until doubled. Bake as usual. This is also good with rye bread. It's literally cheese 'n rye.

When you are shaping the loaf, be sure to fold the dough to make it tight.

WHOLE WHEAT LOAF

Mix 2 pkgs. dry yeast, ¾ c. warm water, and 2 T. honey or brown sugar. Let stand until yeast begins to work.

Cook 1 c. stirred WW flour with 2 c. milk, stirring constantly until thick and smooth.

Add 2 tsp. salt, ¼ c. oil or butter, 2 T. honey or brown sugar, and 1 c. stirred WW flour to cooked flour, mixing well. This should cool the mixture to warm. Then add the yeast and about 3 c. stirred WW flour. Mix well.

Cover and let rise in mixing pan until doubled. Turn out onto floured board and knead until smooth and elastic. Cover and let stand another 15 minutes.

Shape into 2 loaves. Fold edges in to make a tight loaf, place into 2 greased glass loaf pans, and press down into the pans to fit the corners. (If you have trouble with the bread sticking to the pans after it is baked, try lightly flouring the greased pans.) Cover and let rise until doubled. Brush lightly with egg white.

Bake at 400° for 45 to 50 minutes. Remove from pans and cool on cake rack.

TEA RING

Use half of the Stone Mill Bread recipe.

Before cutting the rolls, place rolled-up dough in a circle on a greased cookie sheet. Pinch ends together. With a sharp knife, make cuts about ¾ of the way through, leaving the bottom connected. Make the cuts about an inch apart. Twist each section outward and lay it on its side. Let rise until doubled, then bake and ice.

BUTTER BATTER BREAD

This is a no-knead, light bread. It makes delicious toast.

Mix ½ c. warm water, 1 T. brown sugar or honey, and 1½ pkgs. dry yeast. Set aside until it doubles. It will do this by the time you are ready to mix it into the dough.

Stir 1 c. milk into 2/3 c. stirred WW flour and cook until thick and smooth, stirring constantly. It will be lumpy and stick to the pan, but keep on stirring and cooking and it will smooth out. Put into a large bowl.

Add ½ c. butter or margarine to the hot mixture. Then add 1½ tsp. salt, ¼ c. well-packed brown sugar or honey, 3 eggs, and 1 c. stirred WW flour. Mix well.

Add yeast mixture to flour mixture. Add 2½ c. stirred WW flour. If you have used honey instead of sugar, add another 2 T. WW flour. Mix well. This should be a soft dough.

Cover with a towel and let rise until double. Stir down and let rise another 15 minutes. Stir vigorously again. This stirring takes the place of kneading. I use a table knife, stirring round and round.

Pour oil onto a cookie sheet that has turned-up sides. This oil will keep the soft dough from sticking as you shape it into 2 loaves. Place the loaves in 2 greased and floured glass loaf pans. Let rise until doubled.

Bake at 400° for 35 to 40 minutes. If you have used honey, turn down to 375° after 25 minutes of baking.

Cool on cake racks.

A new cook must learn old methods.
An old cook must learn new methods.
Any good cook is always learning.

◈ ◈ ◈

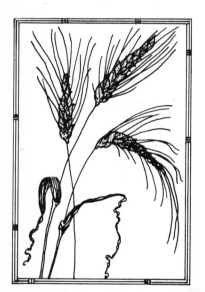

BREAD AND BUTTER PUDDING

Toast enough Butter Batter Bread slices to loosely fill an 8 x 12-inch oblong glass baking dish.

Spread with ¼ c. butter or margarine and place in a baking dish. Set aside.

Beat together 4 eggs, 4 c. milk, ¼ tsp. salt, 1 tsp. vanilla, and ¾ c. well-packed brown sugar. Stir until sugar is dissolved.

Pour over bread, soaking it completely.

Sprinkle with nutmeg.

Bake at 325° for about 45 minutes, or until brown.

Chill before cutting to prevent custard from weeping. Delicious with cream.

HOMEMADE BREAD

No matter how they dress it up . . . Upon the grocer's shelf . . . No bread can ever be as good . . . As what you bake yourself.

O wondrous smell . . . O crisp brown crust . . . O butter melting through . . . And best of all, the happy thought . . . That this was baked by you!

Eleanor Graham Vance

From *IT HAPPENS EVERYDAY* by Eleanor Graham Vance, 1962, Golden Quill Press, Francestown, N. H. Used by permission of the author.

TENDER EGG BREAD

Mix together ½ c. warm water, 1½ pkgs. dry yeast, and 1 T. honey or brown sugar. Let stand until doubled.

Mix 1½ c. water and 1 c. stirred WW flour. Cook, stirring constantly until thick and smooth.

Add 2/3 c. oil, 1 T. salt, 2 T. honey or brown sugar, 3 eggs, and 1 egg white. These additions should cool the batter enough to add the yeast mixture. Mix in well.

Add 4¾ c. stirred WW flour.

Let rise until doubled, then turn out onto floured board, table, or cookie sheet. Knead until smooth and elastic. Let stand 15 minutes, punch down, cut into 8 pieces to braid as Stone Mill Bread, let stand another 15 minutes, then shape. Put on greased cookie sheets.

Let rise until doubled, then brush with 1 egg yolk beaten with 1 tsp. water. Sprinkle with poppy seed.

Bake at 350° for 50 to 55 minutes.

Although this book stresses whole grains as good tasting, you also get the advantage of the full nutrition they offer.

❖   ❖   ❖

Cooking is a creative art—it can bring pleasure, relaxation, and a sense of accomplishment.

A FRIENDLY KITCHEN

I like a friendly kitchen
With colors bright and gay,
A checkered cloth, a lovely dish
Will brighten my whole day.

A flower on the windowsill
Makes me think of spring,
And happy children trouping in
Make my heart begin to sing.

The homey smell of cooking
Can chase the blues away,
Before you know it, you will say
It's such a lovely day.

Esther Betts

LEMON BREAD

Measure everything before mixing.

Take ½ c. well-packed brown sugar out of a full box (pound) and mix with ½ c. lemon juice. This will be the glaze.

Beat together 1 c. oil and the remainder of the box of brown sugar. An electric mixer is good for this.

Add 4 eggs, beating in one at a time.

Mix ½ tsp. salt and ½ tsp. soda with 1 c. buttermilk. Add 3 c. sifted WW flour to egg mixture, alternately with buttermilk, starting and ending with flour. Beat well.

Mix in grated rind of 3 lemons and 1 c. ground pecans.

Pour into 2 greased, wax-paper-lined glass loaf pans.

Bake at 350° for about 50 minutes.

Remove bread from pans to wax paper or foil placed on a cookie sheet. Prick holes on the top of the bread with a toothpick, bring the lemon-sugar mixture to a boil, and spoon over the top of the hot bread, covering it completely. The glaze will run down the sides to the bottom.

Do not wrap the bread until it is completely cold.

NUT BREAD

Stir together 2 c. sifted WW flour, 2½ tsp. baking powder, and ¾ tsp. salt.

Mix 1 c. broken pecans into flour.

Beat together ½ c. oil, ¾ c. mild-flavored honey, 1 egg, ½ c. milk, and ½ tsp. vanilla.

Stir dry ingredients into liquids until well mixed.

Pour into greased, wax-paper-lined loaf pan.

Bake at 350° for 50 to 60 minutes.

Honey burns easily. Watch carefully during the baking period.

VARIATIONS:

For nut bread that is less sweet, reduce honey to ½ c., increase salt to 1¼ tsp., increase milk to 2/3 c., and omit vanilla.

Substitute 1 c. each sifted brown rice flour and oat flour for the WW flour.

DATE-NUT BREAD

Add 1 c. cut dates to recipe for Nut Bread.

```
◆◆◆◆◆◆◆◆◆◆◆◆◆◆◆◆◆◆◆◆◆◆◆◆◆◆◆◆◆◆◆◆◆

        ABBREVIATIONS:

      tsp.—teaspoon
      T.—tablespoon
      c.—cup
      pkg.—package
      WW—whole wheat

◆◆◆◆◆◆◆◆◆◆◆◆◆◆◆◆◆◆◆◆◆◆◆◆◆◆◆◆◆◆◆◆◆
```

BOSTON BROWN BREAD

Mix 1 c. cornmeal, 2 c. stirred WW flour, 1 tsp. salt, 1 T. baking powder, ¾ c. sorghum, 2 c. buttermilk, and 1 c. raisins.

Fill 4 oiled #2 cans half full.

Bake at 350° for 45 to 50 minutes, or until browned.

Delicious with cream cheese, butter, peanut butter mixed with chopped pickles, or with the traditional baked beans.

HONEY BANANA BREAD

Stir together 2 c. sifted WW flour, 2½ tsp. baking powder, and ¾ tsp. salt.

Beat together ½ c. oil, ¾ c. mild-flavored honey, 1 egg, and 1 c. mashed bananas (very ripe for flavor).

Beat flour into banana mixture and add 1 c. broken pecans.

Pour into greased, wax-paper-lined loaf pan.

Bake at 350° for 50 to 60 minutes.

Honey burns easily. Watch carefully during the baking period.

Variation: Substitute 1 c. each sifted brown rice flour and oat flour for WW flour.

BANANA NUT BREAD

Cream ½ c. softened butter or margarine with 1 c. well-packed brown sugar.

Mix in 1 egg, 3 T. milk, and 1 c. mashed bananas (very ripe for flavor).

Stir together 2 c. sifted WW flour, 2½ tsp. baking powder, and ¾ tsp. salt. Add to banana mixture. Beat well.

Add 1 c. broken pecans.

Pour into greased, wax-paper-lined loaf pan.

Bake at 350° for 50 to 60 minutes.

Variation: Substitute 1 c. each sifted brown rice flour and oat flour in place of WW flour. Also add another egg and omit milk.

MUFFINS

CORN MUFFINS

Mix 1 c. sifted WW flour, 2½ tsp. baking powder, and ½ tsp. salt.

Beat together ⅓ c. oil, ¼ c. mild-flavored honey (or ⅓ c. brown sugar; if you use sugar, omit 1 T. of the flour), 1 egg, and 1½ c. buttermilk.

Mix dry ingredients and liquids.

Stir in 1 c. cornmeal.

Bake in greased muffin tin at 400° for about 25 minutes. Let cool 5 minutes for easier removal. Makes 12 muffins.

NOTE: Finely ground cornmeal makes the best muffins. If it is fine enough, try substituting 1 c. cornmeal for the flour.

RYE MUFFINS

Use Whole Wheat Muffin recipe with these changes: Substitute ½ c. rye flour for ½ c. of the WW flour, and add 2 tsp. caraway seed.

NUT MUFFINS

Add to Whole Wheat Muffin recipe ½ c. broken pecans. Mix into the dry ingredients.

> Always mix ingredients thoroughly, unless the recipe specifies otherwise.

CRANBERRY MUFFINS

Mix 1 c. chopped raw cranberries and ½ c. well-packed brown sugar or raw sugar.

Stir together 2 c. sifted WW flour, 2½ tsp. baking powder, and ¼ tsp. salt.

Beat together ¾ c. buttermilk, 1 egg, ¼ c. oil, and ¼ c. well-packed brown sugar or raw sugar.

Make a well in dry ingredients and add liquids all at once, stirring until flour is moistened. Add cranberries, mixing as little as possible.

Bake in greased muffin tin at 400° for 20 to 25 minutes. Makes 12 muffins.

Variation: Substitute 1 c. each sifted brown rice flour and oat flour in place of WW flour.

WHOLE WHEAT MUFFINS

Mix 1-2/3 c. sifted WW flour, 2 tsp. baking powder, and a scant ½ tsp. salt.

Beat together ¾ c. milk (or 1 c. buttermilk), 1 egg, ⅓ c. oil, and 2 T. honey or brown sugar.

Make a well in dry ingredients. Add liquids all at once and stir only until the flour is moistened. Batter will be lumpy.

Bake in greased muffin tin at 400° for about 25 minutes. Makes 9 muffins.

Variation: Substitute 1 c. sifted oat flour and 2/3 c. sifted brown rice flour in place of WW flour.

APPLE NUT MUFFINS

Stir together 1¾ c. sifted WW flour, 2 tsp. baking powder, ½ tsp. salt, 1 tsp. cinnamon, and ¼ tsp. nutmeg.

Beat together 1 c. buttermilk, 1 egg, ⅓ c. oil, and ¼ c. honey (or well-packed brown sugar; if you use sugar, reduce the flour to 1-2/3 c.).

Add ½ c. broken pecans and ¾ c. chopped apples to flour mixture, then pour in liquids all at once and stir until flour is moistened.

Bake in greased muffin tin at 400° for about 25 minutes. Makes 12 muffins.

Variation: Substitute 1 c. sifted oat flour and ¾ c. sifted brown rice flour in place of WW flour.

BUTTERMILK BRANFLAKE MUFFINS

Mix together 1½ c. 40% bran flakes, 1 c. buttermilk, 1 egg, ¼ c. oil, and ¼ c. well-packed brown sugar.

Mix together ¾ c. stirred WW flour, 2 tsp. baking powder, and ½ tsp. salt.

Stir 2/3 c. raisins into flour. Also, ⅓ c. broken pecans can be used if desired.

Add flour to first mixture, stirring only until flour is moistened.

Bake in greased muffin tin at 375° for about 30 minutes. Makes 12 muffins.

BLUEBERRY MUFFINS

Stir together 1-2/3 c. stirred WW flour, 2 tsp. baking powder, and ½ tsp. salt.

Beat together 1 c. buttermilk, 1 egg, ⅓ c. oil, and 2 T. brown sugar or honey.

Make a well in dry ingredients. Pour in liquids all at once and stir only until flour is moistened.

Fold in 1 c. well-drained canned blueberries and 1 T. blueberry juice.

Bake in greased muffin tin at 400° for about 25 minutes. Makes 12 muffins.

SWEET ROLLS

SWEET ROLLS

Mix ½ c. warm water, 1 T. brown sugar or honey, and 1½ pkgs. dry yeast. Set aside.

Mix 1 c. stirred WW flour with 1½ c. water. Cook until thick and smooth, stirring constantly. Then put into a large bowl.

Add to cooked flour ½ c. oil, ½ c. well-packed brown sugar or honey, 1 scant T. salt, and 2 eggs. Mix ½ c. powdered milk into 1 c. WW flour and mix into dough. Next, add the yeast mixture, and lastly, add 2¾ c. stirred WW flour. (If you have used honey instead of brown sugar, add an extra ¼ c. flour.) Mix well.

Let rise in mixing bowl, covered, for about 1 hour or until double in bulk. Stir down well and let rise again. Place on floured board and knead by folding for a few minutes, then shape.

Press half of the dough into a 10 x 16-inch rectangle. Spread with filling. (See filling recipes.)

Roll up, starting with the 16-inch edge. Seal seam by pinching with fingers.

Cut into 1-inch slices by slipping a thread under the rolled-up dough, crossing it over the top and pulling.

Place on a greased cookie sheet, press to make flatter, then let rise until double.

Bake at 375° for 15 to 20 minutes, or until lightly browned.

Ice while hot unless otherwise specified.

NOTE: To freeze sweet rolls, do not ice. When ready to use, heat on a cookie sheet, uncovered, at 350°. Then ice.

Try adding caraway or anise seed to the dough.

FILLINGS FOR SWEET ROLLS

BUTTERSCOTCH ROLLS
Spread 2 T. softened butter or margarine on rolled-out dough. Then spread ⅓ c. well-packed brown sugar over butter. Add broken pecans or black walnuts if desired.

Glaze while hot with the following icing:

Cook 2 T. butter or margarine with ½ c. well-packed brown sugar, stirring constantly, until sugar is dissolved. Add 2 T. milk, stirring in well. Cool. Add ½ to 2/3 c. powdered sugar to make a soft icing.

MAPLE NUT ROLLS
Spread 2 T. softened butter or margarine on rolled-out roll dough. Sprinkle ⅓ c. maple sugar over butter. Add broken pecans.

Glaze when cool with this icing:

Mix together 1 tsp. butter or margarine for each tablespoon of pure maple sugar candy.

CINNAMON ROLLS
Spread 2 T. softened butter or margarine on rolled-out roll dough.

Mix together ⅓ c. well-packed brown sugar and 2 tsp. cinnamon. Spread over butter. Add raisins and pecans if desired.

Glaze while hot with thin powdered sugar and water icing (about 1¼ tsp. water to ½ c. sifted powdered sugar). Or glaze with icing for Butterscotch Rolls.

DATE ROLLS
Spread Date Filling on rolled-out dough. Add nuts if desired. Glaze with any of the above icings.

FILLED ROLLS
See Danish Pastry, Cheese Filling and Fruit Filling.

HOT CROSS BUNS

Use half of the Sweet Roll recipe.

Mix grated peel of ½ orange and ½ lemon with 2 T. honey and cook at medium heat, stirring, for a minute after it boils.

Remove from heat and add 1 T. butter or margarine, ½ tsp. cinnamon, and ½ c. raisins.

Stir into dough, then knead on lightly floured board a minute or two. It shouldn't take long to become smooth and elastic.

Cut into 12 pieces and shape into buns. Place on a greased cookie sheet, with a little space in between. Let rise until doubled. With a sharp knife cut a shallow cross in the top of each bun.

Bake at 375° for 20 to 30 minutes, or until browned.

Ice while hot with thin powdered sugar and water icing. Flavor with 1 tsp. lemon juice. Put more icing in the cross.

BEAR CLAWS

Mix ¼ c. softened butter or margarine, ½ c. well-packed brown sugar, ½ tsp. almond flavoring, and ⅓ c. ground almonds. This is enough for half of the Sweet Roll recipe. Cut into 10 pieces.

Flatten each piece into an oval and spread with almond mixture.

Fold in half and flatten. With a scissor make short cuts into the rounded sides to form the claws. Let rise until double.

Bake at 375° for 15 to 20 minutes.

Ice while hot with thin powdered sugar and water icing, flavored with a small amount of almond extract.

DANISH PASTRY

Cream 1 c. butter or margarine with ½ c. stirred WW flour. Spread to an 8-inch square on wax paper. Wrap and refrigerate to harden again.

Mix ½ c. warm water, 2 pkgs. dry yeast, and 1 T. brown sugar or honey. Set aside.

Stir 1½ c. water into 1 c. stirred WW flour. Cook, stirring constantly, until thick and smooth. (This mixture will stick and get lumpy, but keep stirring and cooking.)

Add to the cooked flour ¼ c. well-packed brown sugar or honey, 1 tsp. salt, and 2 eggs. Mix 1 c. stirred WW flour with ⅓ c. powdered milk and add. Stir in yeast mixture and 2 more cups stirred WW flour. Add 2 extra tablespoons of flour if you have used honey. Mix well. Cover and let stand 15 minutes.

Turn out onto floured board and knead until elastic. Pat out to an 8 x 16-inch rectangle, place chilled butter-flour mixture on half of the dough, and fold the other half over. Wrap and chill in the refrigerator.

Take out of the refrigerator, place on lightly floured board, fold in thirds, then roll out again. Repeat 3 times. Cut into 3 pieces. Keep 2 pieces in the refrigerator while shaping the other.

NOTE: The secrets of making good Danish Pastry are to keep the dough chilled until shaped, and to make the rolls flat.

FILLINGS

CHEESE FILLING

Roll dough into a 10 x 16-inch rectangle and roll up tightly, starting with the 10-inch edge. Cut into 12 slices. Place on cookie sheet and press flat (about ¼-inch thick). Press the bottom of a floured drinking glass into the center of each roll to make a deep depression. Let rise until doubled, then fill with the following:

Beat together 3 oz. cream cheese with ¼ c. honey. Beat in ¼ c. dairy sour cream, ½ tsp. vanilla, ¼ tsp. almond flavoring, and 1 egg.

Bake at 375° for about 15 minutes, or until browned. While hot, glaze lightly around the edges with thin powdered sugar and water icing.

FRUIT FILLING

Prepare dough as for Cheese Filling. In place of the cheese mixture, spoon on some preserves or pie filling, such as in the Cherry Pie recipe. Bake and glaze.

PANCAKES

FRUIT PANCAKES

Beat together 1 c. milk, 1 c. stirred WW flour, and ¼ tsp. salt.

Beat 4 egg whites until stiff, then beat in 4 egg yolks until just mixed through.

Fold eggs into flour mixture.

Bake on ungreased or lightly greased griddle.

Cover with thickened, sweetened raspberries or other favorite fruit.

These pancakes can be spread with the fruit, rolled up, and sprinkled with powdered sugar or served with whipped cream.

Variation: Substitute ½ c. each stirred brown rice flour and oat flour in place of WW flour.

CORNMEAL PANCAKES

Mix together 1 c. yellow cornmeal, ¼ c. stirred WW flour, and ½ tsp. salt.

Add 1¼ c. boiling water slowly, stirring all the time. Add a little more water if necessary to make a medium batter.

Blend in 2 T. oil and 1 tsp. brown sugar or honey.

Beat 2 egg whites until stiff, then add 2 egg yolks, beating until mixed.

Fold eggs into batter.

Bake on ungreased or lightly greased griddle.

NOTE: If the cornmeal is very finely ground, omit the WW flour and increase the cornmeal to 1¼ c.

BUTTERMILK CORNMEAL PANCAKES

Mix together 1⅛ c. cornmeal, ⅛ tsp. salt, and 1½ tsp. baking powder.

Beat together 1 c. buttermilk, ⅓ c. oil, and 2 eggs.

Add buttermilk mixture to cornmeal.

Bake on ungreased or lightly greased griddle.

BUTTERMILK PANCAKES

Mix 1 c. sifted WW flour, 2 tsp. baking powder, and ½ tsp. salt.

Stir 1 T. mild honey into 3 T. oil. Then add 1 c. buttermilk and 2 large eggs. Beat well.

Mix flour into liquids until flour is just moistened.

Bake on ungreased or lightly greased griddle.

Serve with honey and butter mixed together in equal parts.

Variation: Substitute ½ c. each sifted brown rice flour and oat flour in place of WW flour.

BLUEBERRY PANCAKES

Add ¾ c. well-drained canned blueberries to Buttermilk Pancakes.

Serve with this fruit syrup: Mix ½ c. blueberry juice with 1 c. raw sugar and 1 T. lemon juice. Bring to a boil, stirring, and cook until sugar is dissolved.

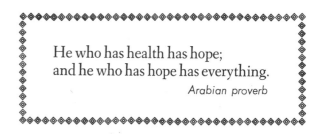

He who has health has hope;
and he who has hope has everything.
Arabian proverb

APPLE PANCAKES

Mix together 1 c. sifted WW flour, 1 tsp. baking powder, ⅛ tsp. salt, ¼ tsp. cinnamon, and ⅛ tsp. cloves.

Cut in 3 T. butter or margarine.

Beat together 1 egg, ⅓ c. milk, 2 T. powdered milk, and ½ c. applesauce.

Add to flour, mixing until moistened.

Bake on ungreased or lightly greased griddle.

Make Fruit Syrup, using apple juice with a little lemon juice.

Variation: Substitute ½ c. each sifted brown rice flour and oat flour in place of WW flour.

WAFFLES

PECAN WAFFLES

Mix 1 c. sifted WW flour, 1½ tsp. baking powder, and ¼ tsp. salt.

Beat together 1 c. buttermilk, ⅓ c. oil, and 2 tsp. brown sugar or raw sugar.

Beat 2 egg whites until stiff, add 2 egg yolks, and beat until just mixed through.

Mix flour into liquids.

Fold in beaten eggs and ½ c. broken pecans.

Bake. Makes 2 or more large waffles.

Strawberry Waffles: Omit pecans and cover baked waffles with strawberries and whipped cream.

Wheatless: Substitute ½ c. each sifted brown rice flour and oat flour in place of WW flour.

There is no spectacle on earth more appealing than that of a beautiful woman in the act of cooking dinner for someone she loves.

Thomas Wolfe

POPOVERS

Place 1 c. milk, ½ tsp. salt, and ¼ c. butter or margarine into a saucepan and bring to a boil, stirring.

Add 1 c. stirred WW flour all at once. Stir vigorously until the dough forms a ball and follows the spoon around the pan. Cool slightly. (I usually put it in a mixing bowl, which helps to cool it.)

Add 3 eggs, one at a time, beating each egg in well.

Divide into 12 greased muffin cups. The dough will still be warm.

Bake at 400° for 35 to 40 minutes. Do not open the oven until the last 5 minutes of baking.

NOTE: These popovers may be reheated, uncovered, on a cookie sheet at 350°.

PANCAKE AND WAFFLE SYRUPS

NATURAL SYRUPS

The natural syrups include honey, maple syrup, and molasses. Try mixing honey and butter together, or honey, butter, and cinnamon to taste.

FRUIT SYRUP

Boil 2½ c. light raw sugar with 1 c. pineapple juice or your favorite juice, until sugar is dissolved.

Add 2 T. lemon juice if flavor is weak.

MAPLE-FLAVORED SYRUP

Boil 2½ c. well-packed brown sugar with 1 c. water until sugar is dissolved. Remove from heat.

Add ½ c. pure maple syrup.

BAKE OVEN

Georgia B. Adams

The old bake oven built
Close to the kitchen door,
Was Grandma's place to bake her bread,
And many goodies more.

We children helped to gather up
The kindling for the fire,
A sample of her baking was
All that we asked for hire.

A paddle, long and wooden, sent
Into the oven's heart
The raised bread dough, the pies, the cakes,
Perhaps an apple tart.

The whiff of ginger cookies or
The fragrant tempting pies;
The smell of bread crust browning, these
I still can realize.

And though the oven boasts
Antiquity today,
I see my grandma baking there
As if 'twere yesterday.

NUTTY DROP DOUGHNUTS

Mix 2 c. sifted WW flour, ¼ tsp. nutmeg, ¾ tsp. salt, and 1 T. baking powder.

Beat together 2 eggs, 6 T. milk, 2 T. oil, and ⅓ c. well-packed brown sugar or raw sugar.

Combine liquids and dry ingredients.

Add ½ c. broken nuts.

Drop by half teaspoonsful into hot oil at about 375°.

Drain on paper towel and roll in powdered sugar or the following mixture:

Mix together ¼ c. brown sugar, ¼ c. powdered sugar, 1 tsp. cinnamon, and ½ tsp. nutmeg.

Variation: Substitute 1 c. each sifted brown rice flour and oat flour in place of WW flour.

GINGERBREAD

Cream together ½ c. butter or margarine with ½ c. well-packed brown sugar. Stir in ⅓ c. honey or molasses (use molasses if you like the old-fashioned flavor). Beat in 1 egg.

Mix together 1½ c. sifted WW flour, ½ tsp. salt, ¾ tsp. ginger, ¾ tsp. cinnamon, and ¼ tsp. cloves.

Add half of the flour mixture to the creamed mixture, beating well. Then add ¼ c. buttermilk. Beat in the rest of the flour.

Bring ⅓ c. water to a boil, add ½ tsp. soda, and add to the batter. Stir well.

Pour into a greased square glass baking pan.

Bake at 350° for about 35 minutes.

Serve with whipped cream.

Wheatless: Substitute ¾ c. each brown rice flour and oat flour in place of WW flour. Add an extra egg.

RAISED DOUGHNUTS

Make Stone Mill Bread dough. When it is ready to shape, use a part of it for doughnuts.

Roll out to ⅓-inch thick and cut with doughnut cutter.

Let rise until very light—this is important.

Fry in deep, hot oil, about 375°. When browned on one side, turn to finish cooking.

Remove to paper towels to drain, then roll while hot in the following mixture: Mix together ¼ c. brown sugar, ¼ c. powdered sugar, 1 tsp. cinnamon, and ½ tsp. nutmeg.

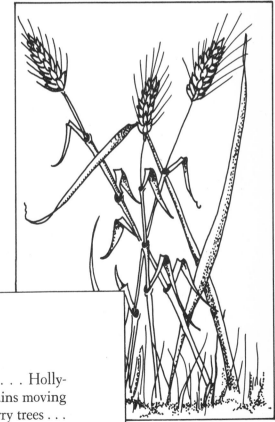

MAKING DOUGHNUTS

Anne Campbell

The kitchen with its well-scrubbed floor . . . Hollyhocks outside the open door . . . The curtains moving in the breeze that blew from Mother's cherry trees . . . The patch of lettuce in the back . . . The plum trees! Oh, there is no lack of memories . . . While here I stand and labor with a practiced hand . . . Making doughnuts.

SHORTCAKES

WHOLE WHEAT SHORTCAKE

Mix together 2 c. stirred WW flour, 3 tsp. baking powder, and ½ tsp. salt.

Cut in ⅓ c. butter or margarine until like coarse crumbs.

Beat together 1 egg, ½ c. milk, and 1 T. brown sugar or honey.

Add liquid all at once to the flour. Stir until just moistened.

Pat to ¾-inch thick on floured board and cut as for large biscuits.

Spread or dip in melted butter.

Bake at 425° about 15 to 20 minutes, or until golden brown.

Serve while hot with strawberries, raspberries, blueberries, peaches, or your favorite fruit. Smother with whipped cream. Try using frozen concentrated pineapple juice, undiluted, as sweetener for the fruit instead of sugar.

Variation: Substitute 1 c. each stirred brown rice flour and oat flour in place of WW flour.

PIECRUST-STYLE SHORTCAKE

Mix together 1 c. stirred WW flour, 1½ tsp. baking powder, and ¼ tsp. salt.

Cut in ¼ c. butter or margarine.

Add ⅓ c. milk, blending just until flour is moistened.

Cut like large biscuits.

Bake at 420° for 15 to 20 minutes, or until golden brown. Makes 4 shortcakes.

Variation: Try buttermilk in place of milk. Also add ¼ tsp. soda.

To make a wheatless shortcake, substitute ½ c. each stirred brown rice flour and oat flour in place of WW flour.

SHORTCAKE TIME

On a blue-sky, sunny day
In the month of June,
I recall the fragrance
Of strawberry bloom.

Bright red nuggets, juicy-sweet,
Hanging from each vine,
Reminded youthful palates
It was strawberry shortcake time.

Juanita Johnson

COFFEE CAKES

STREUSEL COFFEE CAKE

Mix together 2 T. WW flour, ½ c. well-packed brown sugar, 2 T. butter or margarine. When well mixed, add ½ c. black walnuts. This is the filling and topping.

Stir together 1½ c. sifted WW flour, 1½ tsp. baking powder, ½ tsp. salt, ½ tsp. nutmeg, and ⅓ c. powdered milk.

Cut ¼ c. butter or margarine into the flour until it is fine.

Stir ¼ c. black walnuts into the flour.

Mix together 1 large egg, ½ c. milk, ½ c. well-packed brown sugar, and 1 tsp. vanilla.

Add liquids all at once to dry ingredients, stirring only until flour is moistened.

Spread half of the dough into a well-greased 8 x 8 x 1-inch glass baking pan.

Sprinkle with half of the filling.

Spoon the rest of the dough in evenly, and sprinkle the rest of the filling over the top.

Bake at 375° for 25 to 30 minutes. Cool.

VARIATIONS:

Cinnamon Streusel: Omit all black walnuts. Add 2 tsp. cinnamon and ½ c. pecans to filling and topping mixture.

Wheatless: Substitute ¾ c. each sifted brown rice flour and oat flour in place of the 1½ c. WW flour. Also, substitute 2 T. rice flour for the 2 T. WW flour.

ABBREVIATIONS:

tsp.—teaspoon
T.—tablespoon
c.—cup
pkg.—package
WW—whole wheat

BLUEBERRY COFFEE CAKE

Cream together ¾ c. well-packed brown sugar and ⅓ c. butter or margarine. Add 2 eggs and beat well.

Mix 2 c. sifted WW flour with 2 tsp. baking powder and ½ tsp. salt.

Add flour alternately with ⅓ c. milk, starting and ending with the flour. Then stir in 1 c. fresh or frozen blueberries (or well-drained canned blueberries).

Spread in greased 9-inch square cake pan. Sprinkle with another 1 c. blueberries, then with the following topping:

Mix together ½ c. well-packed brown sugar, ⅓ c. stirred WW flour, ½ tsp. cinnamon, and ¼ c. butter or margarine.

Bake at 375° for 40 to 50 minutes.

Wheatless: Substitute 1 c. each brown rice flour and oat flour in place of the 2 c. WW flour. Also substitute ⅓ c. mixed rice and oat flours in place of the ⅓ c. WW flour.

SOUR CREAM COFFEE CAKE

Cream together ½ c. butter or margarine, 1 c. well-packed brown sugar, and 1 T. vanilla.

Beat 2 eggs into the creamed mixture.

Add 1 c. sour cream, 1½ c. sifted WW flour, and 2 tsp. baking powder. Mix all thoroughly.

Spoon a third of this dough into a greased and floured bundt pan.

Sprinkle a third of the following mixture over the dough: ½ c. well-packed brown sugar, 2 tsp. cinnamon, and ½ c. broken pecans.

Repeat this procedure until all the dough and cinnamon mixture is in the pan.

Bake at 350° for 45 minutes.

Allow to cool in pan 5 minutes. Then remove.

FRESH APPLE CAKE

Mix 1½ c. oil (room temperature), 2 c. well-packed brown sugar, 2 large eggs, and 1 tsp. vanilla. Beat well until creamy smooth.

Stir together 2½ c. sifted WW flour, 1 tsp. salt, and 1 T. baking powder.

Add dry ingredients to creamed mixture in small amounts, beating well each time. Finish by hand, as this mixture will be very thick.

Fold in 1 c. black walnuts and 3 c. chopped raw apples.

Bake in greased 9 x 13-inch glass baking dish at 350° for 55 to 60 minutes.

Chill. Serve with whipped cream or ice with Jelled Whipped Cream.

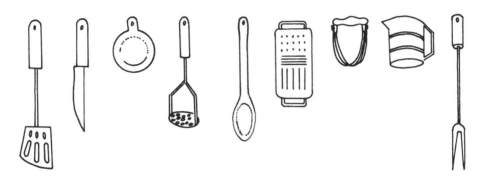

KITCHEN SYMPHONY

The cooking sounds seem musical,
   My kitchen hums a tune . . .
The crunch of sugar in a bowl,
   The slap of batter past a spoon.

I like the whir of beating cream,
   The perk of coffee on the grill;
And lonely would my kitchen seem
   If all its implements were still.

I'd miss the gush of popping steam,
   The hiss of buttered frying pan,
The click of ice cubes 'gainst a glass
   And water swishing as it ran.

I like to hear staccato clicks
   Of chopping, chopping, wood on steel
And in between the dancing ticks
   Of clock notes while I cook each meal.

Doris K. Sutcliffe

RAISIN COFFEE CAKE

Combine 2½ c. sifted WW flour, 1½ tsp. cinnamon, ½ tsp. nutmeg, ¾ tsp. salt, 2½ tsp. baking powder, and 1 c. firmly packed brown sugar, using back of spoon to crush sugar lumps.

Cut in ¾ c. butter or margarine.

Set aside 1 c. of this mixture for topping.

Add 1 c. raisins to the rest of the flour mixture.

Beat 1 c. buttermilk, 1 egg, and 1 tsp. vanilla and stir into flour until it is just moistened.

Pour into greased 9-inch glass cake pan and sprinkle with topping.

Bake at 375° for 35 to 40 minutes, or until brown and done on top. Serve warm.

Wheatless: Substitute 1¼ c. each sifted brown rice flour and oat flour in place of WW flour. Also add an extra egg. Allow the wheatless coffee cake to cool before cutting.

CAKES

LITTLEST ANGEL CAKE

Mix 1 c. sifted WW flour with ¾ c. well-packed brown sugar using the back of the spoon to crush and mix sugar lumps. Put mixture into sifter. (Do not use a double sifter.)

Beat together 1½ c. egg whites, 1½ tsp. cream of tartar, ¼ tsp. salt, 1 tsp. vanilla, and ½ tsp. almond flavoring until stiff but still glossy.

Add ¾ c. well-packed brown sugar in 3 parts, beating well each time.

Use a large spoon in a folding action to make sure everything is mixed well.

Fold in flour with the large spoon, sifting a little over the top and gently folding in.

Pour into ungreased angel food cake pan, smoothing the top.

Bake at 375° for about 35 minutes. Touch the top gently to see if cake is done.

Invert pan and cool completely. Then remove from pan.

VARIATIONS:

Ice with Jelled Whipped Cream, plain or chocolate, or serve with fruit and whipped cream.

You may fill the cake with Jelled Whipped Cream. Slice a thin layer off the top, then hollow out the center. Fill and cover again with the top slice. Chill and serve.

Omit almond flavoring and increase vanilla to 1½ tsp.

Substitute ¼ c. cocoa (or carob powder) for an equal amount of flour, and omit almond flavoring.

Substitute ½ c. each sifted brown rice flour and oat flour in place of WW flour.

JELLED WHIPPED CREAM

Soak 1 tsp. unflavored gelatin in 2 T. cold water.

Melt over hot water.

Pour into 1 c. whipping cream, stirring vigorously.

Chill until firm.

Beat until you have whipped cream.

Spread on cake, fill cream puffs, then refrigerate to set gelatin.

Variations: Flavor with chocolate syrup, carob drink mix, or your favorite flavoring with honey or brown sugar. Maple syrup is good.

CREAM PUFFS

Melt ½ c. butter or margarine in 1 c. boiling water.

Add 1 c. stirred WW flour and ¼ tsp. salt all at once to boiling water, stirring vigorously until smooth and until it forms a ball that follows the spoon around the pan.

Cool slightly.

Add 4 eggs, one at a time, beating each egg in well.

Drop batter onto greased cookie sheets, 6 to a sheet. This recipe makes 12 cream puffs.

Bake at 450° for 15 minutes, then at 325° for 25 minutes.

Cool completely.

Fill with Jelled Whipped Cream. Flavor with chocolate syrup or with brown sugar and vanilla. Refrigerate until cream is set.

PINEAPPLE UPSIDE DOWN CAKE

With a little care, this cake can be made without baking powder. The eggs are enough leavening. It is important to have very large fresh eggs. Beat well and fold lightly. The baking powder was added to insure success.

Mix ¼ c. softened butter or margarine with ½ c. well-packed brown sugar and spread over the bottom of a square glass cake pan.

Place rings of pineapple over butter-sugar mixture, saving juice (see below). Fill in all the spaces between pineapple rings with pecans and red cherries.

Set aside while making cake.

Measure everything before mixing.

Place 3 large egg whites and ⅛ tsp. salt in large bowl of mixer and beat until stiff. Continue beating through next 4 steps.

Add 3 egg yolks.

Pour in scant ⅓ c. boiling pineapple juice, drained from pineapple above.

Add gradually ¾ c. well-packed brown sugar.

Pour in ½ c. oil slowly.

Mix together 1½ c. sifted WW flour and 1 tsp. baking powder.

Fold flour into egg mixture with a large spoon. Sift a little flour over the batter and fold in lightly. Continue this until all the flour is folded in.

Pour into prepared pan.

Bake at 325° about 50 minutes. Touch the top gently to see if cake is done.

Cool 5 minutes before removing from pan.

Variation: Substitute ¾ c. each sifted brown rice flour and oat flour in place of WW flour.

FRUITCAKE

With a little care, this cake can be made without baking powder. The eggs are enough leavening. It is important to have very large fresh eggs. Beat well and fold lightly. The baking powder was added to insure success.

Prepare 3 small 7½ x 3½ x 2¼-inch fruitcake loaf pans, greasing and lining with wax paper.

Measure all ingredients before mixing.

Beat 4 large egg whites and ⅛ tsp. salt in large bowl of mixer until stiff. Continue beating through next 4 steps.

Add 4 egg yolks.

Pour in ½ c. boiling water.

Add gradually 1⅓ c. well-packed brown sugar.

Pour in ½ c. oil slowly. Then add the juice of one lemon.

Mix together 1¾ c. sifted WW flour, 1½ tsp. cinnamon, and 1½ tsp. baking powder.

Fold flour into egg mixture with a large spoon. Sift a little flour over the batter and fold in lightly. Continue this until all the flour is folded in.

Mix ¼ c. WW flour, 2 c. chopped dates, 2 c. raisins, and 2 c. broken pecans. (Use candied fruit if desired.)

Fold fruit and nuts into the batter and pour into prepared pans.

Bake at 350° for about an hour. Touch the top gently to see if the cake is done.

Cool in pans for 5 minutes, then remove to racks to finish cooling.

Store in refrigerator. Do not cut for a week or more, as flavor will develop in the cake and it will also be easier to cut.

Variation: Substitute half brown rice flour and half oat flour in place of WW flour.

WHOLE WHEAT LAYER CAKE

Cream until fluffy ¾ c. butter or margarine, 1⅓ c. well-packed brown or raw sugar, and 1½ tsp. vanilla.

Mix together 2½ c. sifted WW flour, 2½ tsp. baking powder, and ½ tsp. salt.

Add flour alternately with 1 c. milk to the creamed mixture. Start and end with the flour.

Beat 4 egg whites until stiff. Then beat in ¼ c. well-packed brown sugar or raw sugar, and the 4 egg yolks.

Fold the eggs into the batter.

Pour into 3 greased, wax-paper-lined 8-inch layer cake pans.

Bake at 375° for 25 to 30 minutes. Touch top gently to see if cake is done.

Cool 5 minutes in pans, then remove to cake racks to cool completely before icing.

Ice with Brown Sugar Frosting or Coconut Pecan Frosting.

Wheatless: Substitute 1¼ c. each sifted brown rice flour and oat flour in place of WW flour. Reduce butter to ½ c. Ice with the Coconut Pecan Frosting.

BROWN SUGAR FROSTING

Place 1 large egg white, ¾ c. well-packed brown sugar, a dash of salt, ½ tsp. vanilla, and 2½ T. water in top of double boiler over rapidly boiling water.

Beat constantly with rotary egg beater and cook until frosting will stand in peaks.

Remove from heat and beat until thick enough to spread.

Variation: Mix 1 square melted and cooled chocolate through icing.

Caution: If the egg white isn't large enough, it would be better to use more than one, as too little egg white will not carry the chocolate.

COCONUT PECAN FROSTING

Combine 1 c. whipping cream, 1 c. well-packed brown sugar, ½ c. butter or margarine, and 1 tsp. vanilla.

Cook over medium heat, stirring constantly until slightly thickened, about 12 minutes.

Add 1 c. each of moist coconut and broken pecans. Beat until thick enough to spread.

GOOD MEASURE

Sugar, butter, flour, spice
Plus this little rhyme,
Lots of love, a smile or two,
For sure success each time.
3 teaspoons make 1 tablespoon;
4 tablespoons—1 quarter cup;
⅜ cup with 6 tablespoons;
8 fills it halfway up.
1 cup is 16 tablespoons
And 2 cups, as you know,
Make 1 full pint; 2 pints—1 quart,
All ready? Get set—go!

Dan Hoover

DATE-NUT CAKE

Make Whole Wheat Layer Cake batter, reserving 1 heaping T. of the flour to mix with dates.

Add 1 c. each chopped dates and broken pecans.

Pour into greased, wax-paper-lined 9 x 13-inch glass baking pan.

Bake at 350° for 40 to 45 minutes.

Serve with whipped cream or ice with Jelled Whipped Cream.

SPICE CAKE FILLING

Mix ¼ c. cooked, drained raisins, 1 T. raisin juice, ¼ c. firmly-packed brown sugar, 2 tsp. WW flour or rice flour, ½ c. broken pecans, and 2 T. butter.

Bring to a good boil, stirring constantly.

Spread immediately on cake. Let cool while making frosting for the rest of the cake.

CHOCOLATE CREAM CAKE ROLL

Prepare a greased, wax-paper-lined cookie sheet with edges.

Mix 6 T. stirred WW flour, 3 T. cocoa, and ¼ tsp. salt together well. Put into a sifter.

Beat 5 egg whites until stiff. Beat in ¾ c. well-packed brown sugar, 5 egg yolks, and 1 tsp. vanilla.

Fold flour gently into eggs, sifting it over the top.

Spread into prepared pan.

Bake at 400° for about 13 minutes.

Cut off crisp edges and turn onto cloth covered with powdered sugar. Carefully roll up with cloth and cool completely.

Fill with Jelled Whipped Cream and chill.

Variation: Substitute 3 T. each brown rice flour and oat flour in place of WW flour.

SPICE CAKE

With a little care, this cake can be made without baking powder. The eggs are enough leavening. It is important to have very large fresh eggs. Beat well and fold lightly. The baking powder was added to insure success.

Measure all ingredients before mixing.

Prepare three 8-inch or two 9-inch layer cake pans, greasing and lining with wax paper.

Beat 4 large egg whites and ⅛ tsp. salt until very stiff in large bowl of mixer. Continue beating through next 4 steps.

Add 4 egg yolks.

Pour in ½ c. boiling water.

Add gradually 1⅓ c. well-packed brown sugar.

Pour in 2/3 c. oil slowly.

Mix together 2 c. sifted WW flour, 1½ tsp. cinnamon, ¼ tsp. nutmeg, ¼ tsp. cloves, and 1½ tsp. baking powder.

Fold flour into egg mixture with a large spoon. Sift a little flour over the batter and fold in lightly. Continue this until all the flour is folded in.

Pour into prepared cake pans.

Bake at 350° for about 30 minutes. Touch the top gently to see if it is done.

Cool 5 minutes in pans, then turn out on cake racks to finish cooling.

Spread Brown Sugar Frosting between cake layers, on sides, and edges of the top, and Spice Cake Filling on top of cake.

Variation: Substitute 1 c. each sifted brown rice flour and oat flour in place of WW flour.

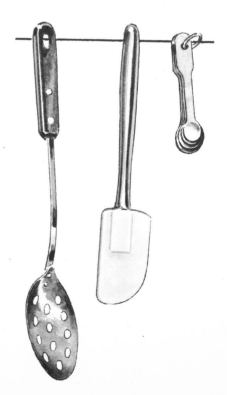

CHOCOLATE CAKE

Measure all ingredients before mixing.

Prepare three 8-inch layer cake pans, greasing and lining with wax paper.

Cream 1 c. butter and 2 c. well-packed brown sugar in large bowl of mixer until fluffy.

Add 2 eggs and beat well.

Sift together 2½ c. sifted WW flour and ½ c. cocoa.

Mix 1 c. buttermilk with 1 tsp. vanilla.

Add flour and buttermilk alternately to creamed mixture, starting and ending with flour.

Add 2 tsp. soda, then ⅞ c. boiling water all at once. Mix.

Pour immediately into prepared cake pans.

Bake at 350° for 30 minutes. Do not open the oven door during the 30 minutes. Touch top of cake gently to see if it is done. If not, turn oven off and let cake stay in oven a few minutes more.

Remove from oven, cool 5 minutes in pans, and turn out onto cake racks to finish cooling.

Ice with 2 recipes of Brown Sugar Frosting—using 1 recipe of chocolate between layers and 1 recipe of plain for sides and top.

Wheatless: Substitute 1¼ c. each sifted brown rice flour and oat flour in place of WW flour. Also, reduce the ⅞ c. boiling water to ¾ c.

GERMAN CHOCOLATE CAKE

Prepare 3 greased, wax-paper-lined 8-inch layer cake pans.

Melt 1 bar German chocolate in ½ c. boiling water and cool.

Cream 1 c. butter or margarine with 2 c. well-packed brown sugar until fluffy.

Blend chocolate, creamed mixture, and 1 tsp. vanilla.

Mix together 2½ c. sifted WW flour, ½ tsp. salt, and 2½ tsp. baking powder.

Add flour and 1 c. buttermilk alternately to creamed mixture. Begin and end with flour. Beat well.

Beat 4 egg whites until stiff, then add 4 egg yolks and beat until mixed through.

Fold eggs into cake batter and pour into prepared pans.

Bake at 350° for 30 to 40 minutes. Touch top gently to see if cake is done.

Cool 5 minutes in the pans, then remove to cake racks to finish cooling.

Frost with Coconut Pecan Frosting between layers and on top.

Variation: Substitute 1¼ c. each sifted brown rice flour and oat flour in place of WW flour.

POUND CAKE

Mix 2¼ c. sifted WW flour, 1 tsp. baking powder, 1 tsp. salt, and 2/3 c. powdered milk.

Beat together well 2/3 c. butter or margarine and 1 c. mild-flavored honey. Then add 3 eggs, 1 tsp. vanilla, ½ tsp. almond flavoring, and ½ c. milk, beating well.

Mix dry ingredients into liquids. Beat well until smooth.

Pour into greased, wax-paper-lined loaf pan.

Bake at 300° for 1½ hours.

VARIATIONS:

Lemon Flavor: Omit vanilla and almond flavorings. Add 1 T. lemon juice and 1 tsp. grated lemon rind.

Chocolate Flavor: Substitute ½ c. cocoa for ½ c. of the flour.

Brown Sugar Pound Cake: Omit honey and add 1¼ c. well-packed brown sugar. Increase milk to 2/3 c.

Wheatless: Substitute 1 c. brown rice flour and 1¼ c. oat flour in place of WW flour.

TENDER ALMOND CUPCAKES

Beat together well about ⅞ c. egg yolks (left from Littlest Angel Cake) with 2 c. well-packed brown sugar. Add ½ c. butter or margarine and cream well.

Mix together 2½ c. sifted WW flour and 2½ tsp. baking powder.

Mix together 1 c. milk, 1 tsp. vanilla, and ½ tsp. almond flavoring.

Add flour and liquid alternately to creamed mixture, starting and ending with flour. Mix thoroughly.

Pour into greased and floured muffin tins. Makes 20 cupcakes.

Bake at 375° for about 20 to 25 minutes.

Cool in pans 5 minutes, then remove to finish cooling.

Variation: Substitute 1¼ c. each sifted brown rice flour and oat flour in place of WW flour.

QUICK 'N EASY DROP BISCUITS

Mix together 2 c. stirred WW flour, 2 tsp. baking powder, ¼ tsp. soda, and 1 tsp. salt.

Add 1 c. buttermilk and ⅓ c. oil, mixing well.

Drop by heaping tablespoonsful onto a cookie sheet. Pat tops even.

Bake at 425° for 15 to 20 minutes.

Variation: Substitute 1 c. each stirred brown rice flour and oat flour in place of WW flour.

CHEESE BISCUITS

Add 4 oz. grated Colby cheese to either Quick 'N Easy Drop Biscuit or Buttermilk Biscuit recipes. Add to the flour mixture.

QUICK 'N EASY CINNAMON ROLLS

Make 1 recipe Quick 'N Easy Drop Biscuit dough. Stir briskly with spoon until dough sticks together rather than to the bowl.

Press out to an oblong about 9 x 14 inches.

Mix together ¼ c. softened or melted butter or margarine, ½ c. well-packed brown sugar, and 2 tsp. cinnamon. Spread carefully on dough.

Roll up starting with the 14-inch edge. Cut into 12 pieces. Lay cut side up on greased cookie sheet.

Bake at 425° for about 20 minutes.

Ice while hot with thin powdered sugar and water icing.

UNLEAVENED BREAD STICKS

Mix 4 c. stirred WW flour and 1 T. salt.

Mix ½ c. oil, 1 c. milk, and 3 T. brown sugar or honey. Add to dry ingredients.

Knead a little and roll into sticks the size of your little finger.

Bake on ungreased cookie sheet at 375° until lightly browned, or about 20 minutes.

BUTTERMILK BISCUITS

Mix together 2 c. stirred WW flour, 2 tsp. baking powder, ¼ tsp. soda, and ½ tsp. salt.

Cut in ⅓ c. butter or margarine.

Add 1 c. buttermilk. Mix through. Do not overmix.

Pat to ¾-inch thick on floured board or cookie sheet.

Cut biscuits and spread or dip in melted butter or margarine.

Place on cookie sheet, with space in between biscuits.

Bake at 425° for 15 to 20 minutes.

Variation: Substitute 1 c. each stirred brown rice flour and oat flour in place of WW flour.

CARAWAY BISCUITS

Add 2 tsp. caraway seeds to the flour mixture in Buttermilk Biscuit recipe.

SPICY BREAKFAST BISCUITS

Add 1½ tsp. cinnamon and ⅓ c. raisins to the flour mixture, and 2 T. brown sugar or honey to the buttermilk in Buttermilk Biscuit recipe. Add nuts if desired.

This makes a delicious meal served with Fresh Fruit Soup.

QUICK YEAST BISCUITS

Mix ¾ c. warm water, 1 pkg. dry yeast, and 1 T. honey or brown sugar. Set aside.

Stir together 2 c. stirred WW flour, ⅓ c. powdered milk, 2 tsp. baking powder, and 1 tsp. salt.

Cut in ⅓ c. butter or margarine, then mix in yeast mixture. Stir well.

Knead (fold) a few times on floured board. Cut and place on cookie sheet, with space in between. Let stand for 15 minutes.

Bake at 425° for 15 to 20 minutes.

ABOUT HONEY

Honey is a natural sweet; it is quickly and easily metabolized.

As you cook with honey, the following points will be helpful:

As a rule, when replacing sugar with honey, substitute an equal amount of honey for sugar, then reduce the liquid in the recipe by 1 T. for each ¼ c. of honey.

Unless you particularly like a strong-flavored honey,

use a mild one so you don't overpower the particular flavor of the food you are baking.

Be sure to mix honey into the recipe well, to make sure it is a part of the batter.

Batter containing honey browns more quickly than batter made with sugar, so watch carefully at the end of the baking time.

Some honey is very thin. These recipes were all tested with the thicker honey.

HONEY PRUNE CAKE

Mix 2 c. sifted WW flour, 1 tsp. baking powder, 1 tsp. soda, ½ tsp. salt, ½ tsp. cinnamon, and ½ tsp. nutmeg.

Beat together ½ c. softened butter or margarine, ¾ c. mild-flavored honey, and ½ tsp. vanilla. Add 2 eggs and beat well.

Stir 2 c. cooked, seeded, cut-up prunes into the honey mixture.

Add half of the flour mixture and mix well.

Mix in ¼ c. juice from the prunes.

Add 1 c. broken pecans to the remainder of the flour, add to the batter and mix well.

Pour into greased and floured bundt pan, smoothing the top.

Bake at 350° for about 55 minutes. Do not cut for 24 hours.

Serve plain or with whipped cream.

Variation: Substitute 1 c. each sifted brown rice flour and oat flour in place of WW flour.

DATE-NUT HONEY CAKE

Make Honey Cake batter, reserving 1 heaping T. of the flour to mix with the dates.

Add 1 c. each chopped dates and broken pecans.

Pour into greased, wax-paper-lined 9 x 13-inch glass baking pan.

Bake at 350° for 40 to 45 minutes.

Serve with whipped cream or ice with Jelled Whipped Cream.

HONEY FRUITCAKE

Make Honey Prune Cake recipe but omit the vanilla and add the juice of ½ lemon.

Add to the flour 1½ c. dried dates and ½ c. raisins along with the nuts.

Increase ¼ c. prune juice to 6 T. prune juice.

Variation: If you like candied fruit in fruitcake, substitute candied fruit for part of dates and raisins.

DRIED FRUIT HONEY CAKE

Cook for 5 minutes ½ c. each dried apricots, prunes, pineapple, dates, and raisins. Let cool, then pour off water (save for Fresh Fruit Soup). Cut apricots and prunes in 3 pieces, discard seeds. Cut pineapple rings into date-sized pieces. Leave seeded dates and raisins whole. Measure 2½ c. prepared fruit. Extra fruit can be added to the Fresh Fruit Soup.

Beat together ½ c. softened butter or margarine, ¾ c. mild-flavored honey, and the juice of ½ lemon. Add 2 eggs and beat well.

Stir prepared fruit into the honey mixture. Add 1 T. fruit juice.

Mix together 2 c. sifted WW flour, 1 tsp. baking powder, 1 tsp. soda, ½ tsp. salt, ½ tsp. cinnamon, and ½ tsp. nutmeg.

Add 1 c. broken pecans to the flour, then add all ingredients to the honey mixture. Mix well.

Pour into greased and floured bundt pan, smoothing the top.

Bake at 350° for about 55 minutes. Remove to cake rack and cool. Do not cut for 24 hours. Keep in a tight container in the refrigerator.

Variation: Substitute 1 c. each sifted brown rice flour and oat flour in place of WW flour.

NOTE: Let your own taste dictate the kinds of dried fruit to use, in your own favorite combination.

ABOUT CAROB

If you are trying to avoid chocolate, of necessity or by choice, try carob. I don't like to think of carob as a chocolate substitute, however, because carob has its own distinctive flavor and should stand on its own merits. These include vitamins, minerals, proteins, and natural sugars.

CAROB OR CHOCOLATE HONEY CAKE

Substitute ½ c. carob powder or cocoa for ½ c. flour in Honey Cake recipe. Let cake cool completely.

Ice with Honey Frosting but omit fruit juice. After cooking, beat in the following mixture: 3 T. carob powder or cocoa mixed with 1 tsp. vanilla and 4 to 5 tsp. water.

HONEY CAKE

Prepare 3 greased, wax-paper-lined 8-inch layer cake pans.

Measure into a large bowl ¾ c. oil, 1½ c. mild-flavored honey, 4 eggs, and 1½ tsp. vanilla. Beat together well until slightly thickened.

Mix together 2½ c. sifted WW flour, 2½ tsp. baking powder, and ½ tsp. salt.

Add half the flour mixture to the honey mixture, then add ½ c. plus 2 T. milk. Add the rest of the flour and beat well.

Pour into prepared cake pans.

Bake at 375° for 25 to 30 minutes. Touch top gently to see if cake is done. Honey burns rather easily, so watch carefully at the end of baking time.

Cool 5 minutes in pans, then remove to cake racks to cool completely.

Spread Date Filling between layers.

Ice with Honey Frosting or with Jelled Whipped Cream.

Wheatless: Substitute 1¼ c. each sifted brown rice flour and oat flour in place of WW flour. Also reduce the oil to ½ c.

DATE FILLING

Beat soft dates (about 2/3 lb.) with 2 T. frozen concentrated orange-pineapple juice and enough water to make a good spreading consistency. Leave it a little thick. Some dates are soft enough so that you can use a rotary beater, others must be done in a blender; in a blender care must be taken not to add too much water.

HONEY FROSTING

Place 2 egg whites, 2 T. frozen concentrated, undiluted orange-pineapple juice, and ¾ c. mild-flavored honey into top of double boiler over boiling water. (You may use the concentrated orange juice or the concentrated pineapple or lemon juice.)

Beat constantly with rotary egg beater and cook until frosting stands in peaks.

Remove from heat and beat until thick enough to spread.

FRUITED BUNDT CHEESECAKE
(With Honey)

Baked in a bundt pan, this cake combines the flavors of cheesecake and holiday fruits.

CRUST

Crush Sour Cream Spritz cookies with a rolling pin until fine (or use Graham Cracker recipe).

Mix 2 c. crumbs with ¼ c. melted butter or margarine. Generously butter a bundt pan. Then, saving ¼ c. for the top, pour crumb and butter mixture around the pan, pressing it over the bottom and partway up the sides. Set aside.

CAKE

Beat together until smooth two 8 oz. packages cream cheese, ¾ c. honey, 1 tsp. vanilla, ½ tsp. almond flavoring, and 4 tsp. lemon juice. Beat in ¼ c. stirred WW flour and ⅓ c. whipping cream. (Use the other ⅔ c. cream to make the Jelled Whipped Cream for the topping.) Mix in ½ c. broken pecans, ½ c. raisins, and 1 c. finely cut-up dates.

Separate 5 eggs. Beat egg whites with ¼ tsp. salt until stiff. Then add yolks and beat well. Fold eggs into the cheese mixture carefully. At first it will seem as though they will not mix easily, but keep on folding and you will have an even dough. Pour into the prepared crust. Sprinkle reserved crumbs over the top.

Bake at 325° for 1 hour 15 minutes.

Remove from oven and let stand in pan 15 minutes, loosening edges as the cake shrinks. Turn out onto plate by laying the plate on top of the pan. Then, holding it all together, turn upside down. Remove pan and allow to cool. Refrigerate. When thoroughly chilled, cover the top with Jelled Whipped Cream. Decorate the top of the cake with drained mandarin orange slices. Spoon the following glaze over the fruit, letting it run down the sides of the cake.

GLAZE

Cook ⅓ c. water with 2 tsp. arrowroot or cornstarch until thick and clear, stirring constantly. Add ½ c. frozen pineapple juice concentrate and stir well. This cools it enough to spoon over immediately.

Chill cake at least 4 to 6 hours before cutting.

Wheatless: Substitute half brown rice flour and half oat flour in place of WW flour.

NOTE: Use the fruit of your choice instead of the orange slices, such as pineapple tidbits or fresh strawberries.

HONEY GRAHAM CRACKERS

Mix 2 c. stirred WW flour, 2 tsp. baking powder, ¼ tsp. salt, and 3 T. brown sugar.

Cut ½ c. butter or margarine into the flour until it is fine.

Mix 2 T. honey with 2 T. milk, then add to the flour. Mix until dough sticks together and does not stick to the pan or to your hands. Knead a dozen strokes.

Roll out between wax paper, a fourth at a time. Put on an ungreased cookie sheet.

Cut with a pizza cutter. Make holes with a toothpick.

Bake at 375° until lightly browned. When the edges start to brown, remove these crackers and continue to bake the rest.

Variation: Substitute 1 c. each stirred brown rice flour and oat flour for WW flour.

OLD-FASHIONED OATMEAL COOKIES

Cream ½ c. butter or margarine with ½ c. well-packed brown sugar until fluffy. The texture of your cookies depends on creaming well.

Beat in 2 eggs and 2 T. water.

Mix together 1 c. sifted WW flour, ½ tsp. cinnamon, and a pinch of salt. (1 tsp. baking powder is optional.)

Add flour to creamed mixture and mix well.

Add 1 c. rolled oats, ½ c. raisins, and ½ c. broken pecans.

Drop by teaspoonful on ungreased cookie sheet.

Bake at 375° for about 15 minutes, or until lightly browned.

Wheatless: Substitute ½ c. each sifted brown rice flour and oat flour in place of WW flour.

To keep that just-baked goodness in cookies, freeze them in tight-sealing plastic containers. It is easy to take out just the amount you want from one of these containers.

HERMITS

Cream 1 c. butter or margarine with 1 c. well-packed brown sugar until fluffy. The texture of your cookies depends on creaming well.

Add 2 eggs and 5 T. orange juice. Beat well.

Mix 3½ c. sifted WW flour with 1 c. cut dates, 1 c. raisins, and 1 c. broken pecans. (2 tsp. baking powder added to the flour is optional.)

Blend flour and fruit into creamed mixture. Mix well and let stand for 10 minutes.

Drop by teaspoonful on ungreased cookie sheet.

Bake at 400° for about 10 minutes, or until lightly browned.

Wheatless: Substitute 2 c. sifted oat flour and 1½ c. sifted brown rice flour in place of WW flour.

PEANUT BUTTER COOKIES

Cream together well ½ c. butter or margarine and 1 c. well-packed brown sugar.

Add 1 egg, ½ tsp. vanilla, 1 T. water, ¼ tsp. salt, ½ c. peanut butter, and 1 c. sifted WW flour, beating well.

Drop by teaspoonful on ungreased cookie sheet. Dip a fork into flour and press the tops of the cookies lightly to flatten and make a crisscross design. Or put through a cookie press.

Bake at 350° for 12 to 15 minutes, or until lightly browned.

Remove carefully, as these cookies are very soft until cooled.

Wheatless: Substitute ½ c. each brown rice flour and oat flour for the WW flour.

PEANUT BUTTER HONEY SANDWICH COOKIES

Beat together ½ c. butter or margarine, 2/3 c. mild-flavored honey, ¼ tsp. salt, and ½ tsp. vanilla.

Add 2 eggs and beat well.

Beat in ½ c. peanut butter and add 1½ c. sifted WW flour. Beat well.

Drop by teaspoonful on ungreased cookie sheet. Dip a fork in flour and press the tops of the cookies lightly to flatten and make a crisscross design. Or put through a cookie press.

Bake at 350° for 12 to 15 minutes, or until lightly browned.

FILLING

Beat together 3 T. butter or margarine, 3 T. peanut butter, and 3 T. mild-flavored honey.

Spread between 2 cookies. Refrigerate. Old-fashioned peanut butter works best. Also, soft margarine will keep the filling from setting. Refrigeration hardens the filling so it won't squash out when you bite the cookie.

Wheatless: Substitute ¾ c. each brown rice flour and oat flour for WW flour.

BUTTER NUT COOKIES

Cream ½ c. butter or margarine with ¾ c. well-packed brown sugar until fluffy. The texture of your cookies depends on creaming well.

Add 1 egg, 2 T. milk, 1 tsp. vanilla, and ½ tsp. salt.

Beat in well 1¾ c. sifted WW flour. Add ½ c. broken pecans.

Drop by teaspoonful on ungreased cookie sheet. Flatten with a floured fork.

Bake at 400° for about 10 minutes, or until lightly browned.

VARIATIONS:

Substitute black walnuts for pecans.

Omit vanilla, add 1 tsp. grated lemon rind and 1 T. of either of the following: lemon juice, frozen concentrated pineapple juice, or orange juice.

Omit nuts, and instead of flattening with a fork, press a pecan half on top, or make an indentation and fill with a little jelly.

Omit nuts, and put two cookies together with a little powdered sugar icing.

For wheatless substitute 1 c. sifted oat flour and ¾ c. sifted brown rice flour in place of WW flour.

CHOCOLATE CHIP COOKIES

Cream ½ c. butter or margarine with ½ c. well-packed brown sugar or ⅓ c. mild-flavored honey until fluffy. The texture of your cookies depends on creaming well.

Add 1 egg and 1 tsp. vanilla. If you have used sugar instead of honey, add 2 T. water. Beat well.

Add 1¾ c. sifted WW flour and mix through. (1 tsp. baking powder added to the flour is optional.)

Mix a 6 oz. package of chocolate chips and ½ c. broken pecans through dough. Let stand 10 minutes.

Drop by teaspoonful on ungreased cookie sheet.

Bake at 400° for about 10 minutes, or until lightly browned.

Wheatless: Substitute 1 c. sifted oat flour and ¾ c. sifted brown rice flour in place of WW flour.

MINCEMEAT COOKIES

Substitute a 9 oz. package of condensed mincemeat, broken in small pieces, for chocolate chips in Chocolate Chip Cookies.

COCONUT ROLLED OATS COOKIES

Cream ½ c. butter or margarine with ½ c. well-packed brown sugar and 1 tsp. vanilla until fluffy. The texture of your cookies depends on creaming well.

Beat in 2 eggs and 2 T. water.

Mix together 1 c. sifted WW flour and a pinch of salt. (1 tsp. baking powder is optional.)

Add flour to creamed mixture and mix well.

Add 1 c. rolled oats, 1 c. soft coconut, and ½ c. broken pecans.

Drop by teaspoonful on ungreased cookie sheet.

Bake at 375° for about 15 minutes, or until lightly browned.

Wheatless: Substitute ½ c. each sifted brown rice flour and oat flour in place of WW flour.

SOUR CREAM SPRITZ

Cream together ½ c. butter or margarine, ½ c. dairy sour cream, and ¾ c. well-packed brown sugar until fluffy. The texture of your cookies depends on creaming well.

Beat in 1 egg yolk, ¼ tsp. salt, and ½ tsp. vanilla. Lastly, beat in 2 c. stirred WW flour. Beat well.

Drop by teaspoonful on ungreased cookie sheet. Press with floured fork to make a crisscross design and to flatten. These can be put through a cookie press.

Bake at 350° for 12 to 15 minutes, or until lightly browned.

Variation: Mix 1 c. raisins into the dough.

Wheatless: Substitute 1 c. each stirred brown rice flour and oat flour in place of WW flour.

POWDERED SUGAR COOKIES

Cream 1 c. butter or margarine and ½ c. powdered sugar until fluffy.

Mix 2¼ c. sifted WW flour, ½ tsp. salt, and 1 tsp. vanilla and beat into the creamed mixture.

Add ¾ c. finely chopped pecans or black walnuts.

Shape into 1-inch balls, lay on ungreased cookie sheets.

Bake at 375° for 10 to 12 minutes.

Roll while hot in powdered sugar, cool, and roll again.

Wheatless: Substitute 1 c. sifted brown rice flour and 1¼ c. sifted oat flour in place of WW flour.

DATE-NUT BARS

Mix together 1 c. sifted WW flour, ¼ tsp. salt, 1 c. broken pecans, and 1 c. dates cut in thirds.

Separate 4 eggs. Beat egg whites until stiff. Gradually add 1⅓ c. well-packed brown sugar, beating. Then beat in egg yolks.

Fold flour into the eggs until flour is moistened.

Spread in greased and floured 9 x 13-inch glass baking pan.

Bake at 350° until firm, about 25 minutes. Sift powdered sugar over the top if desired.

Cool in pan. When cold, cut into bars. These are better the next day.

Wheatless: Substitute ½ c. each sifted brown rice flour and oat flour in place of WW flour.

NOTE: These bars are chewy. If you prefer a cake-like bar, add ¼ c. oil after you have beaten in the yolks.

SOFT SPRINGERLES

Cream together 2/3 c. butter or margarine and ¾ c. well-packed brown sugar until fluffy. The texture depends on fluffiness.

Add 1 egg, ½ tsp. lemon juice, and 1 tsp. grated lemon rind. Beat well.

Mix together 2 c. sifted WW flour, 1½ tsp. baking powder, and ¼ tsp. salt.

Beat flour mixture into creamed mixture alternately with 4 tsp. milk.

Add 1 T. anise seed.

Roll out in powdered sugar. Cut.

Bake at 375° about 12 minutes.

Wheatless: Substitute 1 c. each sifted brown rice flour and oat flour in place of WW flour.

BUTTERY CREAM CHEESE COOKIES

Cream ½ c. softened butter or margarine, 3 oz. cream cheese, and ½ c. well-packed brown sugar until fluffy. The texture of your cookies depends on fluffiness.

Add ½ tsp. vanilla, ¼ tsp. salt, and 1 egg yolk and beat until light.

Add 1 c. sifted WW flour and mix well.

Drop by small teaspoonsful on ungreased cookie sheet. Press tops with floured fork to flatten.

Bake at 350° for about 18 minutes.

VARIATIONS:

Dough may be put through a cookie press if desired.

Substitute 1 tsp. frozen lemon or orange juice concentrate for vanilla, and add ½ tsp. grated lemon or orange peel.

Substitute ½ c. each sifted brown rice flour and oat flour in place of WW flour.

BROWNIES

Cream together ½ c. butter or margarine and 1 c. well-packed brown sugar until fluffy. The texture of your Brownies depends on fluffiness.

Add 2 eggs. Beat well.

Melt two 1 oz. squares of unsweetened chocolate. Add to the creamed mixture.

Add in the following order: 1 tsp. vanilla, ½ c. stirred WW flour, and ½ c. broken pecans.

Spread in greased 8 x 8 x 2-inch pan.

Bake at 325° for 35 to 40 minutes.

Cool and ice with the following icing:

Beat together 1½ squares melted unsweetened chocolate, a pinch of salt, ½ tsp. vanilla, 3 T. milk, and enough powdered sugar to make a good spreading consistency. It should be soft and fluffy.

Cut in squares.

Wheatless: Substitute ¼ c. each stirred brown rice flour and oat flour in place of WW flour.

NOTE: You may substitute 3 T. cocoa and 1 T. butter for 1 square of chocolate.

PUMPKIN PECAN PIE

Place piecrust in a 9-inch pie pan.

Cream 3 T. butter or margarine with ⅓ c. firmly packed brown sugar or raw sugar.

Add ⅓ c. chopped pecans.

Spread over unbaked crust.

Bake at 450° for 10 minutes, remove from oven, and reduce heat to 350°.

PUMPKIN FILLING

Mix together 1½ c. canned pumpkin, 1 tsp. vanilla, 3 eggs, 1 c. firmly packed brown sugar or raw sugar, 1½ tsp. pumpkin pie spice, and ½ tsp. salt.

Scald 1 c. evaporated milk and ½ c. water.

Combine pumpkin mixture with scalded milk.

Pour into prepared crust.

Bake at 350° for 50 minutes, or until center is set but soft. Do not overbake, since custard will set as it cools. Cool completely.

AMERICAN APPLE PIE

Place Tender Piecrust in a 9-inch pie pan and spread with 1 tsp. WW flour.

Mix together ¾ c. well-packed brown sugar or raw sugar, 2 T. WW flour, 2 tsp. cinnamon, ⅛ tsp. nutmeg, and ⅛ tsp. salt.

Fold this mixture through 6 c. peeled and sliced tart apples.

Pack apples into piecrust and sprinkle with 1 T. lemon juice.

Dot with 2 T. butter or margarine, cover with top crust, seal well, and slit.

Bake at 400° for 55 to 60 minutes, or until apples are done. Serve warm.

Wheatless: Substitute rice flour for WW flour.

FRENCH APPLE PIE

Make American Apple Pie recipe. However, when making a double recipe of Tender Piecrust, divide in half before adding the water.

Add ⅓ c. well-packed brown sugar or raw sugar to half and set aside. Add about 2 T. water to the other half and roll as usual. Place into a 9-inch pie plate. Continue with apple filling, then sprinkle with crumbly crust mixture. Bake.

TENDER PIECRUST

FOR A ONE-CRUST PIE:

Mix together ½ c. stirred WW flour, ½ c. oat flour, and ½ tsp. salt. (You can buy oat flour, or grind oatmeal in your blender, making sure it will go through a sifter.)

Cut ¼ c. butter or margarine into flour until the size of tiny peas.

Mix in lightly about 2 T. cold water, sprinkling a few drops at a time over the top and mixing with a fork. When almost mixed through, press into a ball with the fingers.

Roll dough between wax paper, or press into pie pan.

Prick crust with a fork if you bake it without filling.

Bake at 450° for 10 to 12 minutes, or until lightly browned.

This is a good flavored, tender piecrust. Double the recipe for a two-crust pie.

VARIATIONS:

Instead of ½ c. oat flour, use ¼ c. oat flour and ¼ c. arrowroot starch.

Rice flour may be substituted for oat flour.

Oil may be substituted for butter, but the flavor of the crust will suffer. Add oil along with the water.

Wheatless: Substitute rice flour for WW flour.

DEEP DISH PEACH COBBLER

Mix together 2/3 c. well-packed brown sugar or raw sugar, 1 T. lemon juice, and ¼ tsp. almond flavoring. Add 4 c. sliced fresh peaches.

Place in an 8-inch square pan and heat in oven.

Mix together 1½ c. sifted WW flour, 2 tsp. baking powder, ¼ tsp. salt, and 1 T. brown or raw sugar.

Cut in ⅓ c. butter or margarine.

Beat together ½ c. milk and 1 egg.

Add to the flour all at once, stirring until flour is moistened.

Spread over hot fruit. Sprinkle with a little sugar.

Bake at 400° for 35 to 40 minutes. Delicious with cream.

Variation: Substitute 4 c. blackberries for the peaches and omit the almond flavoring.

Wheatless: Substitute ¾ c. each sifted brown rice flour and oat flour in place of WW flour.

CRUMBLY TOP APPLE COBBLER

French Apple Pie without the bottom crust becomes a cobbler. Serve warm with cream.

CRUMB CRUST

Crumble Butter Nut Cookies or Graham Crackers and place 2 c. crumbs on a cookie sheet. Your crust will have a more interesting texture if it is left a little coarsely crumbled.

Toast crumbs lightly under broiler.

Mix ⅓ c. melted butter or margarine with the crumbs, and press into a 9-inch pie pan. Chill.

Variation: Make 1 recipe of Piecrust-Style Shortcake. Crumble and toast as above. Mix ¼ c. brown sugar and ⅓ c. melted butter with toasted crumbs. (This can be made with wheat or wheatless.)

NOTE: Either lemon or vanilla flavor in the cookies is delicious with Strawberry Cream Cheese Pie. Omit the nuts in the cookie recipe if desired.

STRAWBERRY CREAM CHEESE PIE

Beat until smooth 8 oz. cream cheese, 1 c. buttermilk, 3 T. honey, ½ tsp. vanilla, and ½ tsp. almond flavoring.

Soak 1 pkg. unflavored gelatin in ¼ c. cold water. Dissolve over hot water. Beat into cheese mixture.

Chill until firm.

Beat well and pour into Crumb Crust. Chill until firm.

Cover with Jelled Whipped Cream.

STRAWBERRY PIE

Wash and stem 1 qt. strawberries. Drain well.

Mix together 1 T. arrowroot starch (or tapioca starch or cornstarch), ⅓ c. water, ⅓ c. frozen concentrated pineapple juice, and 2 T. honey. Bring to a boil, stirring constantly. Cool slightly.

Mix cooked juice with strawberries and fill baked piecrust. Chill.

Cover with Jelled Whipped Cream.

STRAWBERRY GLAZE

Thaw frozen unsweetened strawberries.

Mix ¼ c. mild-flavored honey and 1 T. arrowroot or cornstarch, then add ½ c. strawberry juice from thawed strawberries and 2 tsp. lemon juice.

Cook juices until thickened, stirring. Cool slightly.

Place thawed and drained strawberries on top of pie and spoon thickened juice over all.

Chill for at least 4 hours before cutting.

NOTE: If you use fresh strawberries, substitute pineapple juice for strawberry juice. Pineapple is good for a change instead of strawberries.

Always follow a recipe exactly the first time. After you know the way it was meant to be done, make any personal changes that you like.

HONEY CUSTARD PIE

Place into a blender 4 eggs, ⅓ c. mild-flavored honey, ¼ tsp. salt, ½ tsp. vanilla, and ⅛ tsp. almond flavoring. Wait to blend until milk is scalded.

Scald 2⅓ c. milk. Start blender on medium speed, and as soon as eggs are thoroughly mixed, pour the hot milk in slowly.

Pour immediately into unbaked crust. Sprinkle with nutmeg.

Bake at 400° for 25 to 35 minutes. It should be removed from the oven when the custard is set but still soft in the center, as it will keep on cooking a little after it is out of the oven. Cool on a cake rack.

NOTE: If you have no blender, use a rotary beater, making sure the honey is thoroughly mixed.

CRUMBLY CRUST MINCE PIE

Make double recipe of Tender Piecrust. Before adding water, divide in half.

Add ⅓ c. well-packed brown sugar or raw sugar and 1 tsp. cinnamon to half and set aside.

Add about 2 T. water to the other half and roll as usual. Place into a 9-inch pie plate. Brush with egg white and slip into the oven for 3 minutes.

Fill with 2⅔ c. prepared mincemeat.

Sprinkle with crumbly cinnamon mixture.

Bake at 425° for 25 to 30 minutes, or until crust is browned. Cool.

QUICK 'N EASY MINCEMEAT

Place into a saucepan 1 qt. tart apples (pared, cored, and chopped), 2 T. butter, 2/3 c. seedless raisins, ½ c. honey, 1 T. lemon juice, 1 T. frozen orange juice concentrate, 1 T. citron, ½ tsp. cinnamon, ¼ tsp. cloves, and ¼ tsp. salt.

Heat to boiling on medium heat, stirring occasionally. When mixture boils, turn to low heat and simmer, covered, for 10 minutes. Then uncover and continue cooking until it is cooked down to where there is very little juice left.

NOTE: Cook several recipes at one time and freeze some for use later.

FRESH FRUIT PIE

Cook 8 large chopped, pitted prunes in ¼ c. water until most of the water is absorbed. Cool.

Mix ⅓ c. undiluted frozen pineapple juice, ⅓ c. water, and 1 T. cornstarch. Bring to a good boil, stirring.

Cut into small pieces 1 fresh peach, 1 banana, and sections of 1 orange.

Mix all together and pour into a baked pie shell.

Cover with Jelled Whipped Cream. Chill.

WHEAT GERM PIECRUST

Stir together 2 c. sifted WW flour with 1 tsp. salt and 1 T. wheat germ.

Cut in 2/3 c. shortening, one half at a time. Cut the first half until it is very fine. Cut the second half to the size of peas.

Dribble 6 to 7 T. cold water over the flour a little at a time, mixing lightly with a fork, and always adding the water where the flour is dry. When all the flour is slightly damp, press together with your fingers to form a ball. Wrap in wax paper and refrigerate while you make the filling.

Divide in half, roll out on lightly floured board, and place in pie pan. If you bake with a filling, follow baking instructions for the filling. Otherwise, prick crust and bake at 425° for 12 to 15 minutes. Cool and fill.

GERMAN MOCHA PIE

Soak 1 envelope unflavored gelatin in ¼ c. cold water.

Measure into a saucepan 1 c. milk, 1 T. instant coffee (dry), 2 T. honey, 1 bar (4 oz.) German chocolate, and the soaked gelatin. Place over medium heat and stir until the chocolate is melted.

Stir 3 beaten egg yolks into the chocolate mixture and cook for another minute.

Remove from heat and add 1 tsp. vanilla, ⅛ tsp. cinnamon, and ¾ c. milk.

Chill in refrigerator until firm, then beat with rotary beater until fluffy.

Pour into baked and cooled crust, such as Pecan Crust or Tender Piecrust.

Top with Jelled Whipped Cream. Chill well before cutting.

CHERRY PIE

Line a 9-inch pie pan with pastry and brush with egg white. Set aside.

Measure 6 c. frozen unsweetened pie cherries and let thaw.

Mix together 2½ T. tapioca starch (or arrowroot or cornstarch), ⅛ tsp. salt, 1 c. well-packed brown sugar or raw sugar, ¼ tsp. almond flavoring, and 1 T. butter or margarine.

Add cherries and bring to a boil, stirring carefully.

Pour while boiling into prepared crust.

Cover with top crust, sealing and crimping edges. Slit top.

Bake at 425° for about 25 minutes, or until crust is brown.

TURNOVERS

PASTRY: This pastry makes a delicious crust for a pie. You can bake part of it as a piecrust and make the rest into turnovers.

Mix together 3 c. sifted WW flour, 2 T. brown sugar, and ¼ tsp. salt.

Cut in 1 c. butter or margarine.

Mix through lightly 1 c. dairy sour cream. When mixed through, stir briskly until the dough sticks together rather than to the pan.

Cover and chill in refrigerator for several hours or overnight.

SHAPING: Make one of the following fillings when you are ready to bake the turnovers. Fillings should be cooled.

Cut the chilled dough into 12 pieces. While you are working with part of the dough, keep the rest chilled in the refrigerator. Place each piece between wax paper and press or roll into a 6-inch circle. Peel away one piece of wax paper and place about 2 rounded T. of filling on each circle. Fold over, but not quite all the way, leaving a small edge to turn up over the other one. Press edge with a fork or fingers to seal and decorate. Turn into your hand to peel the wax paper off the back, then lay on ungreased cookie sheet. Prick top with fork.

Bake at 375° for about 25 minutes. Cool on cake rack. Delicious served warm or cold.

Variation: Substitute honey for brown sugar and add 2 more T. WW flour.

NOTE: These can be filled, wrapped well, and frozen, ready to bake on short notice. Bake at 375° for about 30 to 35 minutes, or until browned.

PECAN CRUST

Measure 1¼ c. pecans and grind them finely.

Mix pecans with 2 T. brown sugar, ¼ c. powdered dry milk, and ¼ c. softened or melted butter or margarine.

Press on bottom and sides of a 9-inch pie pan.

Bake at 400° for 8 to 10 minutes, or until light brown.

Cool and fill with a cream-type filling.

FILLINGS FOR TURNOVERS

MIXED FRUIT
Thaw and drain 1 c. frozen unsweetened blackberries.

Mix and cook until thick ⅓ c. frozen pineapple juice concentrate, 2 tsp. arrowroot or cornstarch, 2 T. raisins, and juice from berries, stirring constantly.

Remove from heat, add drained blackberries and ½ banana, diced.

CHERRY
Make half of the Cherry Pie Filling recipe. You can substitute blackberries, raspberries, or other berries. If the juice seems too thick because the berries have too little juice, add a little frozen concentrated pineapple juice mixed with an equal part of water.

APPLE
Mix together 2 c. apples (peeled, cored, and chopped), ¼ c. brown sugar or raw sugar, ½ tsp. cinnamon, ⅛ tsp. nutmeg, a dash of salt, ½ c. applesauce, and 1 tsp. lemon juice.

MINCEMEAT
Use prepared mincemeat.

MEAT
These make delicious meat pies. You can use leftover chicken, beef, or ham, cubed. Add gravy or a medium cream sauce or undiluted cream soup such as mushroom. If desired, add peas, mushrooms, leftover vegetables, or a bouillon cube. Make these when you have the leftovers, and freeze for a quick meal later.

ALMOND CRUST

Measure 1 c. shelled almonds and grind them finely.

Follow directions for Pecan Crust, substituting the ground almonds for pecans.

If you have a favorite piecrust recipe, try substituting 2 to 4 T. wheat germ for the same amount of flour.

ABOUT BAKING WITHOUT WHEAT

For those who are allergic to wheat
or who just like to try something different . . .

A good wheatless flour is half brown rice flour and half oat flour. (If the recipe calls for 1¾ c. flour, use 1 c. oat and ¾ c. rice, leaning a little heavier toward the oat flour.) The two flours together are better than either one alone.

There are two main considerations to take into account when baking with flours other than wheat flour. First, gluten is noticeably absent. Foods made from these flours are very tender and break easily. Handle them carefully! This is both an advantage and a disadvantage. You will always have a tender cake by using rice and oat flours, and your piecrust problem is in reverse. It is almost impossible to get a tough crust. (In fact, it is a bit too tender. Individual pies are especially easy to make.)

SOUR CREAM COFFEE CAKE

Cream together ⅓ c. softened butter or margarine, 1 c. well-packed brown sugar, and 2 tsp. vanilla.

Beat 3 eggs into the creamed mixture.

Mix together 1 c. sifted oat flour, 1 c. sifted brown rice flour, and 2 tsp. baking powder.

Add half of the flours to the creamed mixture, then 1 c. sour cream and the rest of the flour.

Spoon a third of this dough into a greased and floured bundt pan.

Sprinkle a third of the following mixture over the dough: ½ c. well-packed brown sugar, 2 tsp. cinnamon, and ½ c. broken pecans.

Repeat this procedure until all the dough and cinnamon mixture is in the pan.

Bake at 350° for 45 minutes.

Allow to cool in pan for 5 minutes. Remove to rack to cool completely.

SOUR CREAM BREAD

Beat together 3 T. oil and 2 T. honey. Add 3 eggs and beat well.

Mix together 1 c. sifted brown rice flour, 1 c. oat flour, 1¼ tsp. salt, 2 tsp. baking powder, and ¼ tsp. soda.

Add half of the flour mixture to the egg mixture, blending well. Add 1 c. sour cream, then the rest of the flour. Mix well.

Pour into greased and floured bundt pan or glass loaf pan.

Bake at 350° for 40 to 45 minutes.

Allow to cool in pan for 5 minutes. Remove to rack to finish cooling.

SPOON BREAD

Mix 1 c. yellow cornmeal or corn flour with 1 c. cold milk.

Stir into the above mixture 2 c. scalded milk. Cook until thick, stirring.

Beat 4 egg whites until stiff, then beat in the 4 yolks until just mixed through.

Add 2 T. oil, 1 tsp. salt, and 1 tsp. baking powder to cornmeal mixture, mixing well. Then carefully fold in the eggs.

Pour into greased 1½ qt. baking dish or 6 custard cups.

Bake at 350° for 35 minutes to 1 hour, depending on the size of the bowl. Bake until puffed and brown.

Serve immediately with butter. This can be eaten with any meal. It makes a delicious breakfast dish, with a little honey or maple syrup drizzled over it.

Home is not a house alone,
It's family and friends . . .
The warmth that kitchen gatherings
And a cup of coffee lends.

It's love and understanding,
Blended well with kindliness,
That fills the heart and makes
    the home
A place of happiness.

Beverly C. Willard

BLUEBERRY MUFFINS

Mix together 1 c. sifted brown rice flour, 1 c. sifted oat flour, ½ tsp. salt, and 2 tsp. baking powder.

Beat together 2/3 c. milk, 2 eggs, ¼ c. oil, and 2 T. brown sugar or honey.

Make a well in the dry ingredients and add liquid all at once. Stir until just moistened.

Fold in 1 c. well-drained canned blueberries and 1 T. blueberry juice.

Fill 12 greased muffin cups.

Bake at 400° for about 25 minutes.

NOTE: These muffins can be frozen, then reheated on an uncovered cookie sheet at 350° for 15 to 20 minutes.

FRESH APPLE CAKE

Mix 1 c. oil (room temperature), 2 c. well-packed brown sugar, 4 large eggs, and 1 tsp. vanilla. Mix well at low speed until creamy smooth.

Stir together 1¼ c. oat flour, 1¼ c. brown rice flour, 1 tsp. salt, and 1 T. baking powder.

Add half of the dry ingredients to the creamed mixture, beating well. Then add the rest of the dry ingredients, finishing mixing by hand.

Fold through 1 c. black walnuts and 3 c. coarsely chopped, peeled raw apples.

Bake in greased, wax-paper-lined 9 x 13-inch glass baking dish at 350° for about 55 minutes. If the cake starts to get too brown, turn the temperature down for the last few minutes.

Chill. Serve with whipped cream or cover with Jelled Whipped Cream.

SPICY RAISIN BREAD

Make Sour Cream Bread recipe and add 2 tsp. cinnamon, ¼ tsp. nutmeg, and 1 c. raisins to the flour mixture.

QUICK RYE BREAD

Make Sour Cream Bread recipe but use 2/3 c. each of sifted brown rice, oat, and rye flours instead of the 1 c. each of rice and oat flours. Also, add 1 T. caraway seeds.

WHOLE WHEAT PIZZA

Soak ½ pkg. dry yeast in 2 T. warm water, along with 1 tsp. brown sugar or honey.

Mix together 6 T. warm water, 1 T. oil, ½ tsp. salt, and ½ c. stirred WW flour.

Add yeast mixture and 1 egg. Beat well.

Add 1½ c. stirred WW flour. Make soft dough. Let rise ½ to 1 hour, then knead a few minutes.

Spread half of this dough over the bottom of an oiled 9 x 13 x 1½-inch glass baking dish. This dough cannot be baked in a pan without high sides, as it will bubble out.

Mix 1 c. tomato sauce, 1 T. brown sugar or honey, and about ⅛ tsp. oregano (or to your taste). Spread over dough.

Cover sauce completely with quarter-size hamburger patties. (This can be omitted, or substituted with something you particularly like.)

Sprinkle on ½ chopped green pepper, and 1 small can of drained mushrooms.

Cover completely with thin slices of American cheese or similar cheese.

Bake at 450° for 15 minutes, then reduce heat to 375° and bake until cheese is brown. Cut into squares.

Remove from pan with a pancake turner. This pizza will be very juicy and must be eaten with a fork.

MEAT SAUCE

Brown in skillet 1 lb. hamburger, 1 chopped medium onion, and ¼ c. chopped green pepper.

Add to the meat 2 c. tomato sauce, ¼ c. catsup, ¼ tsp. oregano, 1½ T. Worcestershire sauce, ½ tsp. chili powder, ¼ tsp. curry powder, 1 crushed clove of garlic, and salt and pepper to taste.

Simmer until onion is tender.

NOTE: This sauce can also be served on cooked brown rice or spaghetti. Sprinkle grated Colby cheese over each serving.

QUICK 'N EASY PIZZA

Use Quick 'N Easy Drop Biscuit dough. Pat out individual pizzas on greased pans.

Cover generously with the meat sauce given below. Then cover with grated Colby cheese or similar cheese (or use your own favorite pizza ingredients or those in Whole Wheat Pizza).

Bake at 425° for about 20 minutes, or until brown.

MISCELLANEOUS

ORANGE RICE AND CHICKEN

Cut up 1 frying chicken. Dip in brown rice flour or WW flour and brown in ¼ c. butter or margarine.

Mix together 1½ c. orange juice, 2 chicken bouillon cubes, 2 T. honey, 1 tsp. salt, and 1 tsp. rosemary leaves. Pour over browned chicken. When hot, simmer, covered, for 45 to 60 minutes, or until chicken is tender.

While chicken is browning, bring 2½ c. water to a boil in the top of a double boiler. Add 2/3 c. diced celery, 2 T. chopped onion, 1 sliced carrot (2 carrots if small), and 1 c. brown rice. When it boils again, cover and put over the bottom of the double boiler. Turn down to low heat and cook for 45 minutes. Then add ¼ c. butter or margarine, 1 tsp. salt, ¼ c. frozen orange juice concentrate, and ⅛ tsp. thyme. Cook another 15 minutes.

Serve with the chicken, with the natural chicken gravy on the side.

MUSHROOM RICE AND CHICKEN

Dip and brown chicken as above.

Mix 1 can condensed cream of mushroom soup with 1 can of water and pour over the browned chicken. Simmer slowly for 45 to 60 minutes, or until chicken is tender. Salt and pepper to taste.

While chicken is browning, bring 2½ c. water (use drained mushroom juice as part of the water) to a boil in the top of a double boiler. Add 2/3 c. diced celery, 2/3 c. diced onion, 1 sliced carrot (2 carrots if small), and 1 c. brown rice. When it boils again, cover and put over the bottom of the double boiler. Turn down to low heat and cook for 45 minutes. Then add ¼ c. butter or margarine, ½ tsp. salt, 3 chicken bouillon cubes (dissolved in as small amount of water as possible), and 1 can (4 oz.) sliced mushrooms. Cook another 15 minutes.

Serve with the chicken, with the natural chicken gravy on the side.

BARLEY (Chinese Style)

Soak ½ c. hulled barley (not pearled) in 2 c. water for 1 hour. Bring to a boil and cook in a double boiler for 1 hour. Add ½ tsp. salt and cook another half hour.

Cut into 1-inch pieces 2 c. broccoli, ½ c. green onions (including the tender green tops), 1 c. celery, ½ green pepper, and if available, 1 c. each fresh bean sprouts and snow peas. Add vegetables to 2 c. boiling water along with ½ tsp. salt, one 4 oz. can sliced mushrooms including the juice, and 1 to 2 T. soy sauce. Cook until vegetables are tender but still crisp.

Bone 6 half breasts of chicken and cut into ¼-inch-wide strips with a sharp knife or scissors. Dredge in arrowroot or cornstarch. While vegetables are cooking, brown the prepared chicken in 6 T. butter or margarine.

Combine all and serve at once. Sprinkle soy sauce over the top.

Variation: Brown rice may be used in place of barley. Cook as described in the Brown Rice recipe. Cook 1 c. of the rice.

SALAD SANDWICH (Americanized Taco)

Mix yellow cornmeal with enough water to make as thick as sandwich spread.

Place a small spoonful on heated iron skillet and press out to the size of a flat pancake. Cook until brown on one side, turn and cook until done. Keep warm in oven. Use one of these cornmeal rounds for each serving. The following is enough for 6 servings:

Cook 1 lb. hamburger until done (crumbled). Add catsup and hot sauce to taste.

Mix catsup and hot sauce to taste for an extra sauce to serve on the side if desired.

Place cooked cornmeal on a plate.

Cover with a sixth of the meat, then thin slices of American or Cheddar cheese, or grated cheese.

Top with chopped onion, chopped tomato, and chopped lettuce. Use enough so that you completely cover the meat and cheese.

BROWN RICE

Although you can cook brown rice in a saucepan, I prefer to use a double boiler. It requires less attention and never needs stirring.

Bring 2½ c. water to a brisk boil in the top of a double boiler. Add 1 c. brown rice, bring to a boil again, cover, and place over the bottom of the double boiler, which should be boiling well.

Cook for 45 minutes. Then add 1 tsp. salt and cook 15 minutes longer. Waiting to add the salt makes the rice more tender. (The outer shell of dried beans will also be more tender if you don't cook them with salt or ham until nearly done. A few minutes of cooking with salt is enough.)

Rice polish is the part of the rice grain that is taken off to make white rice. It contains rice germ and is a fine powder that can be added to white rice dishes to put back nutritive values. It can also replace part of the flour in pancakes, muffins, and cakes, and can be added to meat loaf and other foods.

My favorite rice is the golden Italian Avorio, which can be found in health food stores. It has a delicious flavor and texture and is high in nutrition. When cooked, it increases to a greater volume than ordinary rice. You can use 6 c. water to 1 c. rice. It is guaranteed not to stick, and is white when done. This rice is not quick-cooking, but is worth it. Try it as a cereal with a little honey, cinnamon, and milk.

BROWN RICE FOR BEEF

Place in a saucepan 1 can onion soup, 1 can water, 1 2 oz. can mushrooms and juice, 3 beef bouillon cubes, ½ c. butter or margarine, and 1¼ c. brown rice. Bring to a boil and put into a baking dish. Cover.

Bake at 325° for 1 hour. Stir once, after 30 minutes.

Serve with roast beef, steak, or hamburger patties.

ABOUT RAW FOODS

As food is cooked, we see changes in color, in texture, and in flavor. We know that vitamin values are lost, enzymes that aid digestion destroyed, and minerals poured down the drain.

Include raw fruits and vegetables as often as possible, cooking them only when necessary. Fresh vegetable salads are both good for you and a delicious way to serve polyunsaturated oils, such as safflower mayonnaise and salad dressings.

Be sure to try Fresh Fruit Soup. This is an unusual way to serve fresh fruits, as is refreshing Banana Ice. These recipes follow, along with the delightful, partially raw Cereal Medley.

CEREAL MEDLEY

This cereal is partly raw. The rest is only slightly cooked. It contains high quality proteins.

Place 1 T. each of rye grains, millet, barley, and oat groats into a measuring cup. Then put grains and 4 times as much water into blender and liquefy. Stop blender and push the grains that climbed up the sides back down to blend until very fine.

Pour mixture into saucepan with 2 T. raisins and ¼ to ½ tsp. salt. Bring to a good boil, stirring. Remove from heat.

Add to above 1 T. of each of the following: coconut, sesame seeds, sunflower seeds, raw wheat germ, broken pecans, and honey.

Serve with milk.

VARIATIONS:

You may substitute any of these grains: wheat, rice, buckwheat, etc.

Your favorite dried fruit may be used in place of raisins. Cut larger fruit into smaller pieces. Discard seeds.

Any kind of nut can replace the pecans; use rice polish instead of wheat germ. Powdered milk, soybean flour, etc. can be substituted for one of these.

Fresh fruit can also be served with this cereal.

FRESH FRUIT SOUP

Chop and seed prunes. Measure 2/3 c. and place in bowl. Pour 2 c. boiling water over the prunes. Cover and let stand until cold. (If you prefer, leave the prunes whole.)

Add 1 can frozen pineapple juice and 2 cans water.

Add 1½ c. berries (blackberries, blueberries, strawberries).

Choose 1½ c. other fruit such as peaches or pears. Cut, add, and chill.

Add sliced bananas just before serving.

If you want more liquid add more fruit juice. Try to use as much fresh fruit as possible for the enzymes they contain. Your imagination is your only limit for this soup; just be sure to include one dried fruit, one berry, and pineapple and bananas.

Serve with Cinnamon Rolls, Spicy Breakfast Biscuits, or Apple Nut Muffins.

BANANA ICE

Juice 3 oranges and 3 lemons.

Mash and beat 3 ripe bananas with rotary beater. Mix with juices.

Add to above 2/3 c. mild-flavored honey, mixing well. Then add 2 c. water.

Freeze, beating once when almost frozen, if desired.

MILKSHAKE

Try a naturally sweetened milkshake

Place in your blender ¾ c. milk, 1 banana, and ¼ c. pecans.

Blend well.

Or blend your favorite fruit with milk, sweetening with honey to taste.

SALADS

TRY SOMETHING NEW IN SALADS

The next time you go shopping for ingredients to make a tossed salad, look over the produce for the unusual to add to your salad. Try chopped apples or chopped broccoli, thinly sliced Jerusalem artichokes, cauliflower flowerettes, tiny superthin slices of raw beets. Let your imagination lead you.

Don't forget to add deep-green leaves. Green, red, and yellow vegetables make a salad look as good as it will taste, as well as adding considerably to your daily vitamin quota.

A delicious dressing is made by adding a small amount of your favorite dressing to a mashed avocado. This should be thick.

SPINACH SALAD

Wash fresh spinach leaves well. Shred or chop. Measure 2 cups.

Mix together 2 T. salad oil, 1 T. apple cider vinegar (or wine vinegar), 1 tsp. parsley flakes, a few sprinkles paprika, 2 chopped green onions, 2 T. grated cheese, 1 chopped, hard-cooked egg, and salt and pepper to taste.

Toss all together and serve. Vary by using other salad greens or combining several.

GRAPE SALAD

Soak 1 T. unflavored gelatin in ¼ c. cold water.

Bring 1 c. water to a boil, add gelatin, and stir to dissolve.

Add one 6 oz. can frozen grape juice concentrate. Mix well.

Add 2 c. halved, seeded red Tokay grapes.

Chill until gelatin begins to set. Stir to distribute fruit evenly, then place in mold to set.

JELLED FRUIT YOGURT

Make 1 qt. yogurt, following directions accompanying yogurt maker. Save 3 to 4 T. of this to make the next quart of yogurt.

Soak 1 pkg. (1 T.) unflavored gelatin in ½ c. cold water. Then dissolve over hot water. Gelatin will give a desirable texture to the yogurt and keep it from separating. Add another ½ pkg. if you use a lot of fruit, as with the banana or blackberry yogurt.

Mix gelatin and yogurt in blender or mix with rotary beater. This can be chilled until set and topped with fruit, or the fruits can be blended through as follows:

GRAPE OR ORANGE
1 c. jelled yogurt
¼ c. frozen concentrated grape or orange juice, undiluted

Blend together or beat with a rotary beater. Chill until set.

BANANA
1 c. jelled yogurt
1 banana
¼ c. frozen concentrated orange juice, undiluted

Mix in blender. Chill until set.

BLACKBERRY
1 c. jelled yogurt
1 c. fresh or frozen unsweetened blackberries
Honey to taste

Mix in blender. Chill until set.

PINEAPPLE
Frozen concentrated pineapple juice contains enzymes that prevent gelatin from setting. Make a delicious pineapple sundae by topping chilled, jelled yogurt with the undiluted juice before serving.

For a variety of flavors, use other bottled, concentrated fruit juices.

NOTE: This yogurt makes excellent baby food.

Health and money—between these two temporal blessings is this difference:

Money is the most envied but the least enjoyed; health is the most enjoyed but the least envied.

Adapted from Colton

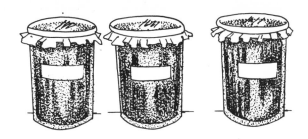

ORANGE MARMALADE

Wash and peel 2 oranges and ½ lemon, leaving most of the white membrane on the fruit. Cut peel into tiny slivers with scissors. Place in a saucepan with ¾ c. water. Bring to a boil on medium heat, stirring occasionally. Then cover, turn to low heat, and simmer 10 to 15 minutes or until tender. Section the two oranges and cut into small pieces, keeping all the juice.

Soak 1 T. unflavored gelatin in ¼ c. cold water.

When peel is tender add one 6 oz. can frozen pineapple juice concentrate and bring to a good boil.

Remove from heat, add soaked gelatin, and stir until it dissolves.

Stir in 1 c. mild-flavored honey. Then add the prepared orange sections, the juice of ½ lemon, and ½ c. frozen orange juice concentrate. Mix well.

Chill until gelatin begins to set. Stir to distribute orange peel and sections. Fill jars and refrigerate. Plastic margarine boxes make good containers for this.

FRUIT CONSERVE

Cook ¼ c. raisins in ½ c. water until raisins swell.

Measure 2 c. frozen unsweetened blackberries. Thaw and crush. This should measure 1 c. when prepared.

Add blackberries to raisins. Also add 1 c. crushed pineapple, ⅓ c. frozen orange juice concentrate, ⅓ c. frozen pineapple juice concentrate, and 1 c. honey.

Soak 1 T. unflavored gelatin* in 2 T. cold water.

Bring fruit to a boil on medium heat, stirring occasionally, and let boil 2 minutes. Then add the gelatin, remove from heat, and stir to dissolve the gelatin.

Chill until the gelatin begins to set. Stir to distribute fruit. Fill jars and refrigerate.

*Always measure the gelatin, as the tablespoon-size packages do not always measure exactly 1 T.

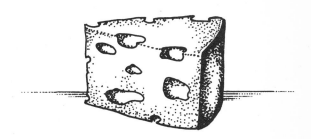

CHEESE AND CRACKERS

FESTIVE BALL 'O CHEESE

Place into a mixing bowl two 8 oz. packages cream cheese (room temperature), ⅓ c. finely chopped green onions (including the tender part of the green tops), 2 finely chopped cloves of garlic, 2 T. finely chopped green pepper, ½ T. parsley flakes, ¼ tsp. Worcestershire sauce, and ¼ tsp. paprika. Beat with a mixer until well mixed.

Grate one 12 oz. package Colby cheese and add it to the cream cheese mixture, mixing through. You will see the colors of the two cheeses and the green vegetables.

Mold into a ball. Decorate with paprika and pecan halves. Chill.

Serve with crackers.

Variations: Add to the above one of the following: chopped pimento, well-drained crumbled bacon, or finely chopped Jalapeño peppers, with a little juice.

CRACKERS

Mix together 2 c. stirred WW flour, 2 tsp. salt, 2 tsp. baking powder, and 2 tsp. brown sugar.

Cut ½ c. butter or margarine into the flour until it is very fine.

Add ⅓ c. milk. This will seem too dry. Knead in the bowl for about a dozen strokes. After kneading, the dough should not be crumbly (if it is, add a little more milk) and it should not stick to the bowl or to the hands (if it does, you have added too much milk).

Divide dough into 4 pieces.

Roll each piece between wax paper as you do piecrust, except make it a little thinner.

Place on an ungreased cookie sheet.

Cut with pizza cutter into squares, diamonds, or triangles and prick with a fork.

Bake at 375° until lightly browned. How long this will take depends on how thick you have rolled the crackers. They will brown around the edges first. Remove those that are done and bake those in the center a little longer.

Variations: Roll caraway seeds, celery seeds, or sesame seeds into the top of the crackers before baking. Or mix 2 tsp. seeds into the dough.

Cheese crackers: Add 2/3 c. grated Cheddar or American cheese.

Bacon crackers: Add ½ c. cooked crumbled bacon.

Wheatless crackers: Substitute 1 c. each sifted brown rice flour and oat flour in place of WW flour.

WANTED . . . TIME
Grace Allard Morse

Time to have my close friends in
　to drink a cup of tea;
Time to read the book of verse
　my sister sent to me.
Time to sort my linens out
　and stack them in neat rows;
Time to look my scrapbook o'er
　and work with rhyme and prose.
Time to bake some muffins
　for the boy who mows our lawn;
Time to listen to the lark
　at morning's early dawn.
Time to cut pink roses
　for a neighbor living near;
Time to plan the garden
　I have wanted for a year.
Time to breakfast leisurely
　and scan the paper through . . .
Time, just to do the things
　I really want to do.

Our sincere thanks to the author
whose address we were unable to locate.

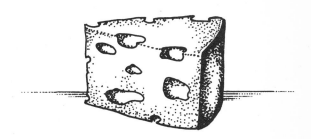

59

THE CHANGING TIMES

John Packham

I think of days that have gone by when mother
  baked her bread.
Back in those days one didn't buy but made
  such things instead.
I could smell the rich aroma from the oven
  that was hot,
And I'll not forget the homemade bread that
  Dad and I once got.
There was something in its flavor, in its added
  bit of zest
That made you feel, beyond a doubt, that homemade
  bread was best.

But times have changed. The womenfolks no
  longer seem to bake.
They buy from stores that stock the things
  commercial bakers make.
The cakes and pies and other things no longer
  have the touch
Of homemade things that man once said he liked
  so very much.
Those good old days when homemade bread was
  wholesome, fresh, and plain
Will far outlive these things today all wrapped
  in cellophane.

Yes, times have changed. And in a way I think
  that it is best.
The woman who once baked her bread has now more
  time to rest.
She need not watch an oven with an ever-watchful eye;
All this has passed and now belongs to days that
  have gone by.
But I, for one, remember and I've more than often said
The better days were back in days when man had
  homemade bread.